MARKS

New Directions In Logo Design
By Jay Vigon

Designed and Edited by
Jay Vigon and Richard Seireeni

Editor: Jay Vigon & Richard Seireeni
Design: Jay Vigon & Richard Seireeni
Publisher: Graphic-sha Publishing Co., Ltd.
Responsible for Publication: Toshiro Kuze
Editorial Coordinator: Nobuhiko Yamada
Editorial Assistant: Rico Samejima
Printing & Binding: Toppan Printing Co., Ltd.

First Publishing, 1986
Copyright © 1986
by Graphic-sha Publishing Co., Ltd.
1-9-12, Kudan-Kita, Chiyoda-Ku, Tokyo 102, Japan
TEL: (03) 263-4318
FAX: (03) 263-5297
TLX: J29877 GRAPHIC

Printed in Japan
ISBN 4-7661-0388-2

To Margo

序　文

　画家．作家．映画監督．彫刻家．我々は皆，いわば料理人である．我々はヴィジュアルな食物をつくる．ロゴデザイナーは，宇宙飛行士が宇宙で食べるような類の食物を作るのである．それは濃縮されており，もしもうまく出来上がったならば，オリジナルのもつ全てのうま味と栄養を備えた良質のものとなる．良いロゴとは，企業の特性を抜粋したものである．或いはまた，理念をヴィジュアルに精製し，表現したものともいえる．あるいは，一挙に書き上げた小説であり，また昨日は紋章，今日は手洗い所の提示，そして明日は政党の旗じるしとして表現されている．それは無言の言語なのである．

　本書は，現代のロゴデザイン界の料理長の一人であるジェイ・ヴァイゴンの作品集である．彼は36才のデザイナー，2児の父であり，かつロサンゼルスにある我々のデザイン事務所では私のパートナーである．だが彼の作品を理解するにはもう少し彼について知っておいた方がよいだろう．ジェイはシカゴ生まれだが，人生のほとんどはカリフォルニアで過ごしている．彼とその双子の兄弟はサンタモニカの学校に通い，まさにカリフォルニア人ならではの独特な環境の中で育った．子供の頃は，La Brea Tar Pits に続く空地で遊び，MGM スタジオの裏側にある人気のない音響ステージに忍びこんだりしていたし，10代では，サーフィンと車，そしていつも身近に感じてきたハリウッドの映像に大きく影響されていた．

　1970年，ジェイはアート・センター・カレッジ・オブ・デザインに入り，広告デザインを専攻した．彼を教えたのは，Jayme Odgers，Roland Young，それに Mortimer Leach という気むずかしい老レタリング講師らで，彼らからは字体と構図の精妙さを学びとった．卒業後，ジェイは妻と兄弟とで主にエンターテイメント産業をクライアントとするデザインスタジオを経営し首尾よく成功をおさめた．彼らのスタジオである Vigon Nahas Vigon はアメリカの有名なレコードジャケットや映画のグラフィックを数多く手がけてきた．彼らはまた斬新で非常に巧妙なロゴを作るという評判を得た．その多くは彼の妻，マーゴ ナハスによる見事なイラストが施されていた．

　私が初めてジェイに会ったのはこの頃のことである．当時，私は Warner Bros. Records でアートディレクターをしていて，レコードジャケットの仕事をするときには，しばしばジェイを使ったものだった．我々が仕事をする上でのつながりや流儀ができていったのは，George Benson，Rod Stewart，Devo，David Lee Roth 等のレコードジャケットを共作したのが縁であった．我々だけのスタジオを開設しようと決意したのもこうした一連の共作がきっかけとなった．スタジオは小規模のままにしておきたいという点ではふたりとも意見が一致していた．今日の広告業界の情況を考えると，大手代理店は増加しつつある小口のクライアントの要望に応えるための設備を整えにくく，効率もよくないということに我々は気づいていた．逆に，かなり読者対象をしぼった定期刊行物やごく専門的なケーブルテレビなどが急速に発達したため，新参の広告業者でもある特殊な市場に手を出せるようなめったにない機会が生じてきていることもわかっていた．ただし広告業界の

中心地であるマディソン街を支える多数の投資はこれらの特殊メディアにまだつぎこまれていなかった．我々はこういった好機を生かして自分達のスタジオを設けたわけで，これまでのところあのときの決断は正しかったようである．

　現在我が社は，種々様々なクライアントのためにデザインを手がけている．今でも時々，レコードのジャケットをデザインすることもあるが，仕事のほとんどは，ファッション産業，コンピュータ・メーカー，映画やテレビの企画，レストランなどに分けられる．我々が製作するものにはカタログ，広告，メニュー，CI 計画，パンフレットなどがあり，時折，ビデオ作品も扱う．これらの作品のコンセプトを作り，デザインをする際にはジェイと私との共同作業になるが，その成功のほとんどは，複雑なメッセージを美しくデザインされたシンボルに変えてしまうことのできる彼の無二の才能に負うところが多い．我が社の成功の礎を認識し，ジェイのファイルにある何百というロゴデザインを再発見したことから，1985年末，我々は彼のロゴデザインに関する本を出版してくれる出版社を探そうと決めるに至った．

　確かに，この本を出版すると決めた我々の思いに絡んで，幾らかの自惚れもあったことは認めざるを得ない．しかし我々をこの本の出版に駆り立てた動機は，現代のロゴデザインが情けない状態にあると見てとったからである．デザイナーとそのクライアントは，"Less Is More"（少ないほど良い）に固執しているようだがこの "Less Is More" はできの良いロゴデザインに備わる2つの重要な特性，すなわち個性と独自性をむしり取ってしまっている．単純な幾可学形を基にした何百という企業のロゴがその最たる例であろう．もしもスタンダードな Helvetica のサブタイトルでもついてないかぎり，互いの区別がつけられないのではないか．

　これとは対照的に，我々のスタジオが目ざすものは，常に顧客毎の個別の問題に対し独自の答えを示していく，コンセプトとしての答えの追求であり続けた．ジェイの作品は，申し分なく概念的であり，しかもそれ以上のものである．彼は，NBC の孔雀や，Richfield の空飛ぶ馬，民主党の象徴のロバなどのロゴに見られる冒険心とユーモアを再び輝かせてきた．Gotcha Sportswear，David Lee Roth や George Lucas といった様々なクライアントのために施した彼のデザインは，A.M.Cassandre，Karl Schulpig，その他20世紀初頭のヨーロッパのデザイナー達の妙技を彷彿させる．彼はその実験的手法，しゃれっ気，奇抜さ，個性において彼ら先駆者達と共通している．

　本書とこれに含まれる一群の作品とが，過度に単純化されて無趣味なデザインに片寄った30年間の流行に刺激を与え，転換をもたらすことがあれば幸いである．この本は味けなく無味乾燥な答えしかないごったがえした市場に対して個性を尊重する為に作られた料理本である．我々は，若いデザイナーや革新的なクライアントがこの本に触発されて自分達のブランドにスパイスを加え，すばらしいデザインを求めて新たな調理法を生み出すことを心から望んでいる．

——リチャード・セイリーニ

Introduction

Painters. Writers. Movie Directors. Sculptors. We're all cooks. We make visual food. Logo designers make the kind of food that astronauts eat in space. It's concentrated. And if it's made right, it has all the taste and nutritional qualities of the original. A good logo is the essence of a company's personality. It is also the visual distillation of an idea. It's a novel in one stroke. It's yesterday's coat of arms, today's restroom sign and tomorrow's political banner. It's an unspoken language.

Marks is about the work of Jay Vigon, one of the master chefs of modern logo design. He's a thirty-six year old designer, father of two and my partner in our Los Angeles based design firm. But to understand his work, it's helpful to know more. Jay was born in Chicago, but has lived in California most of his life. He and his twin brother attended school in Santa Monica and grew up in the environment that is unique only to true Californians. As a kid, he played on the abandoned lots next to the La Brea Tar Pits and snuck onto empty sound stages on the backlot of MGM Studios. His teenage ambitions were molded by surfing, the automobile and the ever-present shadow of Hollywood.

In 1970, Jay entered Art Center School of Design and majored in Advertising Design. His teachers included Jayme Odgers, Roland Young and a crusty, old lettering instructor, named Mortimer Leach, who taught him the subtleties of letterform and composition. After graduating, Jay, his wife and his brother ran a successful design studio catering primarily to the entertainment industry. Their studio, Vigon Nahas Vigon, was responsible for designing many of America's best known album covers and movie graphics. They also began to earn a reputation for innovative and exceptionally well crafted logos, many of which were brilliantly illustrated by his wife, Margo Nahas.

It was during this period that I first met Jay. At the time, I was Art Director at Warner Bros. Records and would often hire Jay to work on album cover projects. It was our collaboration on covers for George Benson, Rod Stewart, Devo and David Lee Roth which crafted the working relationship and style that led to our decision to open our own studio. Jay and I both agreed that we wanted to keep our studio small, and we realized that in today's advertising environment, large agencies are not equipped nor effective in servicing the growing number of smaller clients. We also realized that the explosion of highly targeted periodicals and narrow-cast cable television has created unprecedented opportunities for new advertisers to reach very specific markets; but missing in this specialized media was the mega-buck fee, the life's breath of Madison Avenue. We designed our studio to take advantage of these opportunities, and that decision has so far proved successful.

Today, our firm designs for a wide variety of clients. We still do an occasional album cover, but most of our work is divided among the fashion industry, computer manufacturers, movie and television projects and restaurants. Our products include catalogs, advertisements, menus, corporate identity programs, brochures and, occasionally, video productions. Although Jay and I collaborate on conceptualization and design of these pieces, much of their success is due to Jay's unique ability to translate complex messages into beautifully designed symbols. The recognition of this cornerstone in our firm's success and the discovery of hundreds of logo designs in Jay's files led us to a decision in late 1985 to seek a publisher for a book about Jay's logo designs.

Admittedly, there was a certain amount of ego involved in our decision to publish this book, but our overriding motivation came from our view that modern logo design is in a sorry state. Designers and their clients seem to have gone on a "Less Is More" diet that's stripped away the two most important attributes of successful logo design: individuality and uniqueness. The clearest example can be seen in the hundreds of corporate logos that are based on simple geometric forms. If it weren't for the standard Helvetica subtitle, it would be hard to tell them apart.

In contrast, our studio ambition has always been the pursuit of conceptual solutions that produce unique answers to a client's specific problems. Jay's work is completely conceptual and more. He has rekindled the humor and spirit of adventure that we used to see in logos like the NBC peacock, the Richfield flying horse and the Democratic Party's donkey. His designs for such diverse clients as Gotcha Sportswear, David Lee Roth and George Lucas recall the best of A.M. Cassandre, Karl Schulpig and other European designers of the early twentieth century. He shares their love for experimentation, quirkiness, eccentricity and personality.

Marks and the body of work it contains will hopefully forecast a change in direction and stimulate a shift in a three decade trend toward overly simplified and sterile designs. It's a cookbook for individuality in a marketplace crowded with bland and sometimes tasteless solutions. Our hope is that young designers and innovative clients will be inspired to add their own brand of spice and create new recipes for great design.

—Richard Seireeni

Rick Seireeni
in the studio
Feb. 1986

Jay Vigon

Los Angeles, California

Author's Notes:
A Personal Approach

People often ask me, "Where do you get your ideas?" I take this as a compliment. However, the question seems to allude to the existence of a magic box from which I merely pull the appropriate solutions. Or, that I possess some sort of power that takes the place of work. Where I get my ideas and how I work, are difficult concepts to explain.

Explaining what I do is to intellectualize a process that is actually a mixture of emotion, logic and constantly changing influences. Creativity knows no clear cut path. There are many twists and turns along the way. Experimentation, artistic expression and abstract conceptualization come into play during the creative process. I always keep the television and radio on to help monitor the mercurial trends in fashion, entertainment, politics and business. The whims and biases of a client must also be taken into account. The blend results in a design solution. The variables and uncertainties are part of what makes this work interesting for me. The challenge with each project is to give life to a concept rather than provide a piece of decoration.

Each job begins with the rather pure and idealistic goal of achieving something fresh, new and great! The first thing I do is open a dialogue with the client. It's actually a question and answer session. What is the person like who is buying your product? What have you done in the past that has or has not worked? How do you evaluate the personality of your business? The "Q" and "A" segment is a very important part of the creative process. You can never have too much client input—the more you know about a client and his product, the more parameters a client can set, and the more a problem will dictate its own solution. Peeling away the layers of a given problem to reveal an answer is what distinguishes the conceptual from the decorative. The worst kind of assignment is when a client says, "Do anything you want—be creative." That is the time to restate your questions and press for answers. The client must always be part of the design problem. My work improved most when I was able to free myself from the art school fantasy that my conceptual skills would someday be so refined as to be above client reproach.

Before turning to the drawing board, I translate my head full of client information into visual notes. The process sometimes starts in my shower or lying in bed with a sketch pad after the kids have gone to sleep. An idea might hit me on a Saturday morning between innings of a Dodger game. Time and place are not important—the thoughts come and go continually. What is important is to get the ideas out quickly and unedited.

Evaluating the thumbnail sketches is the hard part. Self-criticism is a discipline. The questions start again, only this time they are directed inward. "Am I keeping my client's needs in mind? Am I settling for the ordinary? Am I doing my best work?" In order to achieve my initial goal, I must stay experimental, flexible and original. There is a tendency to become overly attached to early ideas. Once these rough ideas have been assessed and I am convinced that all relevant possibilities have been covered, I will bring from two to five of the choices (perhaps more) to a semi-finished level for the first client presentation.

When it comes to presentation, I'll be the first to admit that this portion of the process is not my forte. Fortunately, most of the clients that hire the studio are familiar with our work and like what we produce. The clients are usually looking forward to an unexpected solution. Hopefully, the initial input is apparent in the final design. If a client is visually sophisticated, they may communicate their likes and dislikes easily. If not, I will have to give the images verbal support in order to help the client understand the direction, and to elicit responses from them. Either way, getting feedback on all the ideas presented is important. The information will be used for further exploration if none of the ideas presented are approved. In rare instances, the client doesn't like anything, no matter how many sketches I come back with. A lack of rapport is usually the reason—it's not a clash of egos. Dealing with the client's ego is part of the design problem. Most clients do appreciate the in-depth thinking that has gone into the solution of their problem. What I find myself stressing the most to a client is to encourage them to accept something that they have not seen before—to try and not be afraid of leading the way rather than playing it safe. Even the most radical images are assimilated quickly by the public and become a part of the general design language.

The "finish" part of the process is the most tedious, but I find it oddly therapeutic. All the thinking is over with. The idea has already established the final form of the design. I need to take the time to do a perfect inking, which could take an hour or two days. I turn on the radio and take whatever time I need to take.

The process I have described can be emulated, but the end product is uniquely my own. My work is both a synthesis of ideas and information based on what I have learned about a client, and is a blending of variables as they relate to my own life experience. The sum total of all I have encountered is what I give to a project. In this respect, my work is singular. It is unique to my system of filtering out a life full of sense and memories. The more open I am to my thoughts and feelings, the more the creative process takes on a fluid nature.

With this book, I want to relate not only a sense of process and style, but a purpose. Each and every logo is designed to be different and custom-crafted to a particular need, and is not interchangeable with any other, nor is it the product of some preconceived notion. Just as a person's voice or fingerprints are unique to themselves, a client should be able to hold a mirror up to his logo and see a reflection of himself, not the designer.

I am often asked if I am afraid I will run out of ideas. It is not likely. I would have to run out of assignments first.

デザインへのアプローチ

"どこからアイディアが浮かんでくるのか？"と私はよく人から聞かれる．私はこれを賛辞だととっている．しかしながらこの質問は，まるで魔法の箱でもあって，そこから私はただ単に適当なソリューションを引き出しているだけのようにもとれる．或いは，仕事を代わりにしてくれるようなある種の力を私が持っているとほのめかしているようでもある．どこから私がアイディアを得て，どうやって仕事をするのかは，説明しがたいコンセプトである．

私が行っている事を説明するのは，実際に感情，論理，常に変化する周囲の影響物とが交錯している過程を知性化することである．創作する事に明確な近道などない．その途中には紆余曲折があるわけだ．創作の進行中に，実験的手法や芸術的表現，抽象的な概念化が行われ始める．私はいつもテレビやラジオをつけておいて，ファッションや催し物，政治，ビジネスの分野の活発な動きを傍受するのに役立てている．クライアントの気まぐれや偏見もまた頭に入れておかねばならない．こういった要素を混ぜ合わせた結果が，デザイン・ソリューションに現われる．可変性や不確定さがあるから，この仕事はおもしろい．企画毎に伴う挑戦は，一片の飾り付けをするというよりむしろ，コンセプトに生命を与えることである．

仕事はどれも新鮮で，目新しくて，素敵な何かを達成するといったかなり純粋で理想的な目標から始まるのだ．私が最初にすることは，クライアントとの対話である．これは実際に質疑応答のセッションという形をとる．"貴社の製品を買い求めるのはどんな人達なのか？""これまでに効果のあったこと，或いはなかったことは？""貴社の事業の性格をどうとらえているか？"等質疑応答の部分は，創作の進行にとり非常に重要な要素である．クライアントの情報入手はいくらしてもしすぎることはない．クライアントとその製品について知れば知るだけ，クライアントはより多くのパラメーターを設定できるし，問題はおのずと解決への道をたどるだろう．答えを明らかにするために，与えられた問題をひとつひとつあたっていくことが，装飾的なものから概念的なものを見分けることなのである．最悪な仕事とはクライアントが"やりたいようにやってくれ——創造的なのを頼む"と言ってきたときである．こんなときこそ，いま一度質問をし，答えを迫るわけである．クライアントは常にデザインの問題に不可分な役割でなければならない．いつの日か，クライアントの非難の言葉など及ばないほど私のコンセプト上の技術は洗練されたものになるのだ…などという美術学校時代の幻想から抜け出すことができたときに，私の仕事は一番はかどるのだった．

ドローイング・ボードに向かう前に，私はクライアントの情報でいっぱいになった頭をビジュアルなメモに移しかえる．仕事の進行は，時にシャワーを浴びている最中や，子供達が寝静まってからベッドにスケッチ用紙をもちこんで寝転びながら始まることがある．土曜の朝のドジャースの試合中にアイディアがひらめくことだってありうる．場所や時間はあまり重大なことでなはない——イメージはひっきりなしに浮かんだり，消えたりするものだ．大事なことはアイディアをすばやく引き出して，手を加えぬままにしておくことだ．

サムネイル程度のものを評価するものは，困難な作業である．自己批判は鍛練だと思っている．再び問いかけが始まるが，ただ今度の質問は心の中へ向けられるものである．"私はクライアントの要望を心に留めているだろうか？""一般的な表現方法に妥協してしまっただろうか？""私は仕事に全力投球しているだろうか？"私は最初の目的を達するため，実験的で，柔軟で，創造的であり続けなければならない．最初に浮かんだアイディアに必要以上に執着するようになる傾向がある．ひとたび，こういったラフ・スケッチが評価されて，関連する全ての可能性を検討し終えたならば，選択支のうち2点から5点（或いはこれ以上）のものを第1回のクライアント・プレゼンテーションに向けて半ば仕上げの段階までもっていくことになる．

プレゼンテーションについて言えば，進行上のこの部分ばかりは私の得意ではないことをあっさり認めざるをえないだろう．幸い，我々のスタジオを使ってくれるクライアントのほとんどは我々の仕事をよくわかっているし，我々の製作するものを気に入ってくれている．クライアントは，たいてい思いがけないソリューションを期待しているものだ．最初のインプットが最終のデザインではっきり表われていることが望ましい．もしもクライアントがヴィジュアルな面で洗練されていれば，自分達の好みをわかりやすく伝えてくることだろう．もしそうでない場合，クライアントがデザインの傾向を理解しやすいようにし，またクライアントの反応を引き出すために，デザインに言葉の上での補足を与えてやらなければならなくなる．どちらにせよ，提示した全アイディアについてのフィードバックを得ることは重要である．もし提示したアイディアのどの1点も受け入れられなかった折には，更に深い調査のために情報が使われることになる．稀なことだが，どんなにたくさんのスケッチを携えていってもクライアントがどれ一つ気に入らない場合がある．たいていは心の通い合いに欠けていたからである．エゴの衝突ではない．クライアントのエゴを

扱うのもデザインの問題の一部である．ほとんどのクライアントは，彼らの問題の解決を探っていくような深層思考のよさを認めている．最もクライアントに強調しようとしているのは，かつて見た事のない何かを受け入れるよう彼らを促すことであり，無難にこなすよりも試してみて，むしろ先端を行くことを恐れないようにすることである．最も過激と思われるようなイメージでさえ，世間はすぐに理解し，受け入れてしまうし，一般的なデザイン言語の一部になってしまうのである．

プロセスの"最終仕上げ"部分が一番退屈である．奇妙な考えだが私はこれを治療のようなものと考えている．全ての思考が終る．アイディアはすでにデザインの最終的な形を固めている．完全なスミ入れをするのに時間をとらねばならない．1時間ですむこともあれば2日かかることだってありうる．私はラジオをつけて，必要なだけの時間をとるのである．

これまで述べてきた過程はまねのできるものかもしれないが，最終結果はあくまでも私のものである．私の作品は，私がクライアントについて聞き知ったことに基づく情報と，アイディアの両方が統合されたものであり，また私自身の人生経験に関わるにつれ変わりゆく物々が混り合ったものである．私がめぐりあったすべての物事の集大成が，一つ一つの企画に私が託せるものである．この点で私の作品は無二のものである．感覚と記憶に満ちた人生から必要なものをふり分け取り出すという私特有のやり方である．私が自分の考えや感情に率直であればあるほど，創作の進行はより流動性を帯びてくる．

この本で私は，仕事のプロセスやスタイルについてだけでなく，その目的についても語りたいと思っている．それぞれどのロゴも特定の要件に応じ，注文で製作され，同じでないようデザインされる上，他のどんなロゴにも取り換えられないし，またどこかで既出となった観念からの製作物でもない．人の声や指紋がその人それぞれに唯一のものであるようにクライアントは自分の注文したロゴに鏡をかざして，デザイナーのではなく，自分自身の影を見ることができて当然であろう．

私はよくアイディアの種がきれはしないか心配にならないかと聞かれる．そんなことがあるとは思えない．まず私は割り合てられた仕事をやりつくさなければならないだろうし．

——ジェイ・ヴァイゴン

Bourgeois Communist Party
Public Service Message
What if the Communists threw
a party…
Client: Vigon Seireeni

Bourgeois Communist Party
公共事業のメッセージ
共産主義者がパーティーを催したら
一体どうなるか？
(C)：Vigon Seireeni

The Skull
Design Firm Logo
One of two main logos for our
company. It was designed to
get attention.
Client: Vigon Seireeni

The Skull
デザイン会社のロゴ
自社のため考えた正ロゴ2点のうち
の1つ．人目をひくようにデザイン
された．
(C)：Vigon Seireeni

Gotcha Sportswear
紳士用スポーツウェア会社の正ロゴ
1985年，我々は有名なカリフォルニ
アのサーフウェア・メーカーである，
Gotcha社のために新しいロゴをデ
ザインするよう依頼された．下絵は，
半人半魚といった水に関係のあるキ
ャラクターへと自然に展開していっ
た．いろいろな工夫・改良を重ねて，
ロゴには我々の初期の頃の字体が組
み合わされ，完成となった．Gotcha
社は新しいロゴを取り入れるにあた
り，幾つか制限をつけていた．しか
し，このキャラクターの持つ大層な
魅力に，社内の人間も顧客も動かさ
れ，そういった制限はすぐさま取り
払われてしまった．スタッフ達によ
り，このロゴには愛情がこめられ
"Moses"（モーゼ）という呼び名が
ついた．興味深い話として当初のキャ
ラクターは三又の"ほこ"をたず
さえた状態のデザインだった為大手
デパート数社が，それでは悪魔的
な印象を与えると言うので懸念した．
そこで我々は，三又の"ほこ"を旗
とやりの絵に変更したのであった．

(C)：Gotcha Sportswear

16

Gotcha Sportswear
Men's Sportswear Company
    Master Logo
In 1985, we were asked to
design a new logo for Gotcha,
the famous California surf-
wear manufacturer. The preliminary sketches seemed to
naturally evolve into an
aquatic character, half man
and half fish. After several
refinements, the logo was
combined with one of our ear-
lier type designs and was
finalized. Gotcha had some
reservations about introduc-
ing a new logo, but those were
quickly dispelled by the enor-
mous appeal this character
had within the company and
with their customers. It was
affectionately named ''Moses''
by the staff.

It's interesting to point out
that the original character was
designed holding a trident,
but some of the larger depart-
ment stores were nervous
about the possibility of satanic
interpretations. We changed
the trident to a flag and staff.
Client: Gotcha Sportswear

Gotcha Sportswear
紳士用スポーツウェア会社
我々のスタジオが衣料メーカーとま
すます係わり合っていくにつれて,
あるブランドに対し一つ以上のマー
クをデザインするよう依頼されるこ
とになった. こういった企業, 特に
スポーツウェア会社はロゴに関して
ものすごい興味をもっている. 彼ら
の商売の大部分は, Tシャツにプリ
ントされたグラフィック, ラベル,
タッグやステッカーを伴うことにな
る. Gotcha Sportswear の例では一
般的な CI として, 前ページに見られ
るマスター・ロゴをデザインした.
この見開きのページに示されている
のは, さらに専門化した分野での要
求に応え, デザインした2次的なロ
ゴである. 補助用のロゴをデザイン
するときは常に, その企業の全社的
なアイデンティティを頭に入れてと
りかかる. それらはオリジナルテー
マを比喩したものである. マーチャ
ンダイジングの価値に加え, こうい
ったロゴにより, 流行に敏感な企業
は柔軟性や選択の好みを巧みに市場
戦略に取りこみ操ることが可能とな
るわけだ.
(C)：Gotcha Sportswear

Gotcha Sportswear
Men's Sportswear Company
As our studio became increasingly involved with clothing manufacturers, we were asked to design more than one mark for a line. These companies, especially the sportswear companies, have a tremendous appetite for logos. Much of their business involves printed graphics on T-shirts, labels, hang tags and stickers.

In this example for Gotcha Sportswear, we designed the master logo shown on the previous page for the company's general identity needs. The logos shown on these pages are secondary logos designed for more specialized needs. The secondary logos are always designed with a company's overall identity in mind. They are metaphors on the original theme. In addition to the merchandising value, this enables trend-sensitive companies to engineer flexibility and choice into their marketing strategies.
Client: Gotcha Sportswear

Shirt Label Design
Men's Sportswear Company
Client: Gotcha Sportswear

Shirt Label Design
紳士用スポーツウェア会社
(C)：Gotcha Sportswear

T-shirt and Fabric Design
Men's Sportswear Company
Client: Gotcha Sportswear

T-shirt and Fabric Design
紳士用スポーツウェア会社
(C)：Gotcha Sportswear

Surf Contest Patch
Men's Sportswear Company
Client: Gotcha Sportswear

Surf Contest Patch
紳士用スポーツウェア会社
(C)：Gotcha Sportswear

Gotcha Sportswear
Catalog Cover Design
This logo was designed for
one of their spring catalogs
and was later used in an
advertising campaign.
Client: Gotcha Sportswear

Gotcha Sportswear
カタログの表紙のデザイン
このロゴは春もののカタログのため
にデザインされ，後に広告キャンペ
ーンの際，使用された．
(C)：Gotcha Sportswear

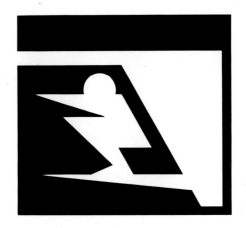

Gotcha Pro
Surfing Contest Logos
In 1986, Gotcha planned
a surfing contest in Hawaii.
They requested some ideas
for a logo that they could use
for merchandising. These were
a few of the designs that I
submitted.
Client: Gotcha Sportswear

Gotcha Pro
サーフィンコンテストのロゴ
1986年，Gotcha 社はハワイでサー
フィン大会を企画した．彼らは，マ
ーチャンダイジングにも用いること
ができるようなアイディアをいくつ
かロゴ用に欲しいということだった．
これらは私が提出したデザインのう
ちの数点である．
(C)：Gotcha Sportswear

Rad Man
Men's Sportswear Company
Another surf motif, but this
time in a primitive style.
Client: Gotcha Sportswear

Rad Man
紳士用スポーツウェア会社
別のサーフィン型モチーフ．ただし
今回のは初歩のスタイル．
(C)：Gotcha Sportswear

The Magic Of Fitness
ホリデイ・ヘルス・スパのコンベン
ション用ロゴ
ヘルス・スパのフランチャイズ店の
オーナー達のコンベンション用の下
絵である. 人間の姿態の美しさをた
たえるというとらえ方によってこの
会合のテーマに専心した.
(C)：J. Walter Thompson
（AD）：Kathy Kosai

The Magic Of Fitness
Holiday Health Spa
    Convention Logo
These were the preliminary
sketches for a convention of
health spa franchise owners.
I tried to concentrate on
the convention's theme by
celebrating the beauty of the
human form.
Client: J. Walter Thompson
Art Director: Kathy Kosai

The Magic Of Fitness
ホリデイ・ヘルス・スパのコンベン
ション用ロゴ
ヘルス・スパのフランチャイズ店の
オーナー達のコンベンション用のた
めの最終的なデザインは，コンベン
ションのテーマを文字どおりに解し
たものであった．初めはこのデザイ
ンがあまりにもセクシーすぎると考
えられていたが，結局，受け入れら
れた．
(C)：J. Walter Thompson

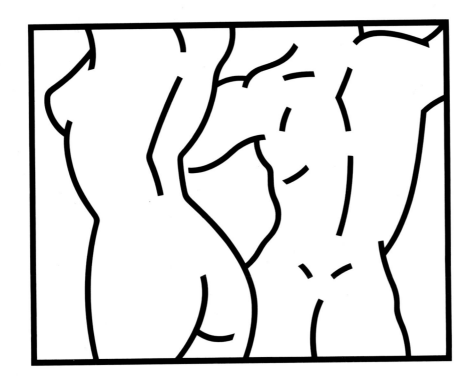

The Magic Of Fitness
Holiday Health Spa
Convention Logo
The final design for this convention of health spa franchise owners was a literal interpretation of the convention's theme. The final design was originally thought to be too sexual, but was eventually accepted.
Client: J. Walter Thompson

The Champp
プロモーション用ロゴ
ボクシングとオカルト的なものから
思いついたもう一人の自己のイメー
ジ.
(C)：Vigon Seireeni

The Champ
Promotional Logo
An image of my alter ego
inspired by boxing and the
occult.
Client: Vigon Seireeni

Style Up
Women's Sportswear Company
One was too hard.
One was too soft.
And one was just right.
Client: Breton Industries

Style Up
婦人用スポーツウェア会社
1点は堅すぎたし，もう1点は柔ら
かすぎた．残り1点がまさにぴった
りだった．
(C)：Breton Industries

Killing Time
Promotional Logo
I did this logo one day when I
was killing time.
Client: Vigon Seireeni

Killing Time
プロモーション用ロゴ
暇つぶしをしていたとき，このロゴ
ができた．
(C)：Vigon Seireeni

Kick Axe

レコードのタイトルデザイン

このロゴには，勢い盛んなヘビーメタル音楽に欠かせないあらゆる要素がとりこんである．いかにも金属的で，不吉な印象や脅威を感じさせる．ヘビーメタル音楽に狂喜する若者に難色を示す親達が不平を鳴らすこと請け合いである．

（C）: Star Kamand

（I）: Margo Z. Nahas

Kick Axe
Album Title Treatment
This logo contains all the
necessary ingredients for
a successful heavy metal
trademark. It's metallic, sinister and intimidating, and
guaranteed to elicit groans
from disapproving parents.
Client: Star Kamand
Illustrator: Margo Z. Nahas

Crazy From The Heat
  The Movie
Movie Title Treatment
One of many title treatments
developed for David Lee Roth's
movie project.
Client: CBS Productions

Crazy From The Heat
  The Movie
映画のタイトルデザイン
David Lee Roth の映画企画向けに製
作されたものの１つ.
（C）: CBS Productions

Carrera
Album Cover Design
This design was commissioned by my partner before we established our design firm and while he was still the Art Director at Warner Bros. Records. The record company didn't want to acknowledge the multi-racial mixture of the band, but still wanted a tribal feeling. I drew it with a stick.
Client: Warner Bros. Records
Art Director: Richard Seireeni

Carrera
レコードジャケットのデザイン
このデザインは，現デザイン事務所の設立前に，私のパートナーであるリチャードがまだ Warner Bros. Records でアートディレクターをしていた頃に製作依頼されたものである．当時クライアントは，このバンドが多人種構成によることをあまり良く思っていなかった反面，デザインには民族調のタッチを望んでいた．これはスティックで描いたもの．
（C）: Warner Bros. Records
（AD）: Richard Seireeni

Deep in the Heart Of Country
Music Division Logo
This logo was designed to be
used with all Warner Bros.
Country Music promotions. It
was one of the first jobs that
Rick and I collaborated on
while he was their art director.
Client: Warner Bros. Records
Art Director: Richard Seireeni
Illustrator: Margo Z. Nahas

Deep in the Heart Of Country
音楽のジャンル別用ロゴ
このロゴは Warner Bros. のカント
リー音楽プロモーションの統一ロゴ
としてデザインされたものである.
リチャードが Warner のアートディ
レクターを務める傍ら, 私と組んで
製作した最初の作品である.
（C）: Warner Bros. Records
（AD）: Richard Seireeni
（I）: Margo Z. Nahas

C.I.A.
Editorial Illustration
This piece was done for an
article about the C.I.A. for
Oui Magazine.
Client: Oui Magazine
Art Director: Jim Kiehl
Illustrator: Margo Z. Nahas

C.I.A.
エディトリアル
この作品は、雑誌 "Oui" の C.I.Aに
関する記事にあわせて作られたもの
である.
(C) : Oui Magazine
(AD) : Jim Kiehl
(I) : Margo Z. Nahas

The First Deadly Sin
Movie Title Treatment
This treatment was developed
for a murder mystery starring
Frank Sinatra. I wanted the
logo to look like it was written
in blood. Rejected.
Client: Filmways Pictures Inc.
Art Director: Bob Rembert

The First Deadly Sin
映画のタイトルデザイン
このデザインは Frank Sinatra 主演
の殺人ミステリー映画のため出され
たもの．私としては，ロゴが血染め
で書かれた様にしたかったのだが，
不採用になった．
（C）：Filmways Pictures Inc.
（AD）：Bob Rembert

Noel Boutique
Charity Fund Raising Event
This charity event involved
the closing of a street in
Beverly Hills and turning it
into an outdoor restaurant. I
wanted to convey the feeling
of a French sidewalk cafe.
Client: Child Help U.S.A.

Noel Boutique
チャリティイベント
このイベントでは，ビバリー・ヒル
ズの街並を，一部通行止めにして，
屋外レストランに仕立てていた．私
は，フランス風の道沿いのカフェの
雰囲気を伝えたいと思った．
(C)：Child Help U.S.A.

Maxus
Album Title Treatment
In addition to everything that
I do for our studio, I also
paint. Sometimes I get an
opportunity to bring this style
into my logo designs. Maxus
was a Jazz/Rock band that
required a softer edged, yet
progressive solution for
their cover.
Client: Warner Bros. Records

Maxus
レコードのタイトルデザイン
仕事場での作業にとどまらず，自分
でも絵を描く．時には，この種の表
現を私のロゴデザインにとりこむこ
ともある．Maxus は，ジャズ／ロッ
クバンドで，彼らのジャケットには，
穏やかではあるがしかし何か進んだ
解釈がほしいとのことだった．
（C）：Warner Bros. Records

Jump Street
Album Title Treatment
Jump Street was a title treatment for an R&B group. It's a
slang expression that means
''The Beginning.'' I borrowed
from Jackson Pollock in order
to create the sense of energy
just before the Big Bang.
Client: Warner Bros. Records
Art Director: Richard Seireeni

Jump Street
レコードのタイトルデザイン
Jump Street は、リズム＆ブルースの
グループのタイトルデザイン例.「始
まり」や「出発点」を意味する俗語
的表現である. Big Bang の直前に在
る勢いの感じを出したいと思い,
Jackson Pollock の絵から借りた.
（C）: Warner Bros. Records
（AD）: Richard Seireeni

Animimotion, Strange Behavior
アーティスト名とそのレコードのタイトル
私達が思いついたデザインは，森林を思わせ，かつおとぎ話の世界のようなものであった．私はロゴがレコードのテーマと合致し，しかも単独のロゴとしても十分通用するものでなくてはと思っていた．あまりに変わった出来だったせいか，バンドの連中は，難癖を付けようとしたが，結局このまま採用された．
（C）: Polygram Records
（AD）: Bill Levy

Animotion, Strange Behavior
Recording Group and Album
  Title
The album design that we
came up with was woodsy and
fairy-tale like. I wanted the
logo to work with the album
theme and still be able to
stand on its own. It was such
an unusual solution that the
band was searching for a reason not to like it, but couldn't.
Client: Polygram Records
Art Director: Bill Levy

Pasha
Recording Company
I made two of the letterforms
in this logo look like smoke
drifting up from a water pipe.
Client: Pasha Music
  Organization
Illustrator: Margo Z. Nahas

Pasha
レコード会社
このロゴでは，水パイプから吹き上
ってくる煙の様なものを2つの文字
で表現した．
（C）: Pasha Music Organization
（I）: Margo Z. Nahas

Heaven
Album Title Treatment
I wanted to combine the word ''heaven'' with threatening imagery so it would more closely reflect the title of the album, ''Where Angels Fear To Tread.'' As a departure from the standard chrome, I asked Margo to render this one as inlayed enamel. I liked it a lot, but the record stiffed.
Client: Browning Management
Illustrator: Margo Z. Nahas

Heaven
レコードのタイトルデザイン
私は "Heaven" という言葉に, "Where Angels Fear To Tread"（天使が畏れて踏み入れぬ所）という何か脅威を与える様なイメージを持たせたかった. このデザインにはよくあるクロム仕上げをやめて, エナメル象眼を施すよう Margo に頼んだ. 私自身は大変気に入っていたが, レコードの売り上げは伸びなかった.
(C) : Browning Management
(I) : Margo Z. Nahas

Dance Mix
Special Dance Album Series
I was looking for a new way to
show motion.
Client: EMI Records
Art Director: Henry Marquez

Dance Mix
ダンス音楽のレコード・シリーズ
躍動感の表現に新鮮さを求めてみた.
（C）：EMI Records
（AD）：Henry Marquez

Prince, Purple Rain
Recording Artist and
    Album Title
This was originally commissioned as a logo for the movie,
"Purple Rain." The mark
was later adapted for use on
Prince's album of the same
name. If I had known that it
was to be used so extensively,
I would have charged more.
Client: Warner Bros. Records
Art Director: Ed Thrasher

Prince, Purple Rain
アーティスト名とレコードのタイトル
ル
これはもともと，映画"Purple Rain"
に用いるロゴとして製作依頼された
もの．後になって，Prince の同名の
レコードに使用されることになった．
これほど広範囲にわたり利用される
とわかっていたら，もっとデザイン
料を請求しておくべきだった．
(C)：Warner Bros. Records
(AD)：Ed Thrasher

Stone Ground
Album Title Treatment
The client had requested a
techno-organic look. This is
as close as I could get.
Client: Warner Bros. Records
Art Director: John Cabalka
Illustrator: Margo Z. Nahas

Stone Ground
レコードのタイトルデザイン
クライアントは，テクノ調の仕上げ
を注文してきた。出来る限り，その
要望にそって作ったのがこれである.
(C) : Warner Bros. Records
（AD）: John Cabalka
（I）: Margo Z. Nahas

Ted Nugent
Album Title Treatment
Ted Nugent had been looking
for a logo for some time and
had gone through about half
a dozen designs before I met
him. Naturally, I was a little
uneasy about the presentation,
and his expression of approval
was a welcome one. He sat
back on the couch and said,
''This is a Mother Fucker.''
Client: Ted Nugent

Ted Nugent
レコードのタイトルデザイン
Ted Nugent はしばし適当なロゴを
探していたようで，私に会う前にす
でに5，6作検討していた．もちろ
ん，このロゴを披露するには幾分，
不安はあったが，彼の満足気な表情
はありがたいものだった．彼はソフ
ァーでくつろぎ，一言「こりゃ，
Mother Fucker だぜ．」
（C）: Ted Nugent

THE
ART
OF
THE
EMPIRE
STRIKES
BACK

The Art of the
　　Empire Strikes Back
本のタイトル・デザイン
このタイトルは，映画，「スターウォ
ーズ—帝国の逆襲」の製作で用いら
れた特殊効果や裏話について書かれ
た本のため作られたもの．右の下絵
は最終的なロゴを描き上げるまでの
過程を示すもので，この本が映画完
成に至るまでを明らかにしていく有
様を彷彿させている．
（C）：Lucasfilm Ltd.
（I）：Peter Greco

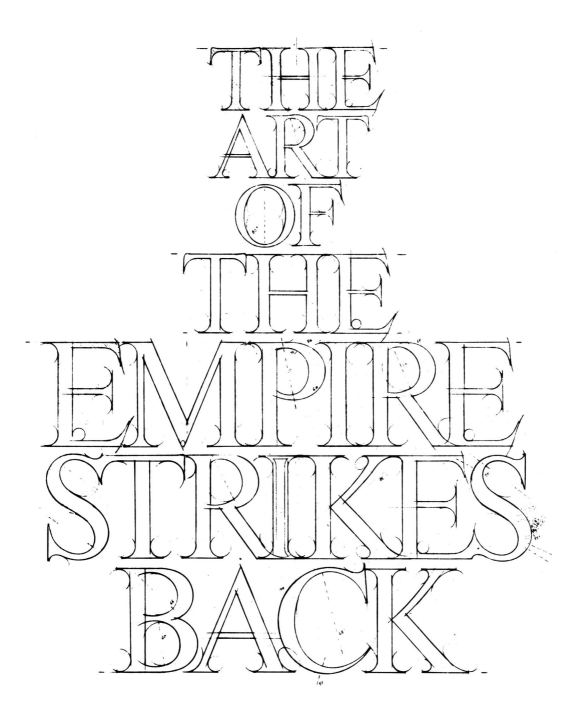

The Art of the
  Empire Strikes Back
Book Title Treatment
This title was created for a book about the behind-the-scene artistry and special effects used to create this Star Wars film. The sketch on the right shows the construction used to create the final logo, just as the book revealed the construction of the film.
Client: Lucasfilm Ltd.
Illustrator: Peter Greco

ZYLOS

Zylos
紳士用スポーツウェアの会社
このデザインは様々に展開されたが,
基本的には,ギリシャ風の雰囲気と
いう統一モチーフ.
(C):Amy Greenberg

ZYLOS

Zylos
Men's Sportswear Company
The designs were all over the
place, but basically had a
Greek feeling.
Client: Amy Greenberg

Brigati, Lost In The
 Wilderness
Recording Group and Album
 Title
I wanted the logo to look like
vines and leaves, but I've for-
gotten why.
Client: Elektra Records
Illustrator: Margo Z. Nahas

Brigati, Lost In The
 Wilderness
アーティスト名とそのレコードタイ
トル
理由は忘れてしまったが，ロゴをつ
る草や葉に見立てたいと思った.
（C）: Elektra Records
（I）: Margo Z. Nahas

The Dove
Children's Charity
    Organization
This charity was organized to
provide funds for a home for
battered children. The dove is
the universal symbol for
peace. In this case, peace in
the home.
Client: Friends of Child Help

The Dove
子供のためのチャリティ機関
このチャリティは，虐待された子供
の家を設立する基金を用立てする目
的で組織された．鳩は，平和を表わ
す万国共通のシンボルである．ここ
では，家庭の安らぎを表現している．
(C)：Friends of Child Help

FM Music Ltd.
レコード会社
　このレコード会社の社名は，"fre-
quency modulation"（周波変調放送）
の頭文字からきている．彼らの音楽
は，FM ラジオ局のリスナーが対象
である．私はこのロゴを持ってあち
こち回ったが，特にどれか1つ選ぶ
という訳でもなかった．クライアン
トが右にある一点を選んだ．人間を
抽象的に型どったもので，東洋風だ
が，本当の意図は進歩的かつ自然な
感じに見せるところにあった．
(C) : Evros Stakis

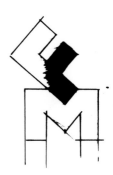

FM Music Ltd.
Recording Company
The name of this record company derives from the initials for "frequency modulation." Their music was targeted for FM radio station listeners. I was all over the place on this one and didn't have any particular preference. The client picked the one on the right. It's an abstraction of a man. It looks oriental, but the real intention was to look progressive and spontaneous.
Client: Evros Stakis

Robert Bane Publishing Inc.
Art Publisher's Copyright Seal
The client is a publisher of
limited edition fine art. He
needed a symbol that could be
embossed into each edition,
without detracting from the
image. The lion motif was
chosen because the client
related to the association.
Client: Robert Bane
Publishing Inc.

Robert Bane Publishing Inc.
美術出版会社の著作権シール
クライアントは，限定版の美術書を
扱う出版業者である．イメージを落
とすことなく各版に浮き出し刷りで
きるようなシンボルを必要としてい
た．ライオンのモチーフは，クライ
アントがライオンみたいだったから．
彼に会いすぐさまこれが浮かび，自
分の意図をすぐに理解してくれた．
（C）: Robert Bane Publishing Inc.

Robert Bane Publishing Inc.
Art Publishing Company
This was a proposal for the
company logo. I was still
working off of the lion motif
which was so successful for
the copyright seal. The more
abstract nature of this piece
was not as well received.
Client: Robert Bane Publishing
    Inc.

Robert Bane Publishing Inc.
美術出版会社
これは社用ロゴとして提案したもの.
著作権シールで功を奏したライオン
のモチーフで私は再度やり抜こうと
した. ただこの作品はより抽象色が
濃かったこともあり, 前作ほどうけ
なかった.
（C）: Robert Bane Publishing Inc.

Malibu Beach Club
洋服の小売り店
アメリカで最も有名なビーチタウン
にある洋服店. 採用となった右のロ
ゴは, 見方によりサングラスとも,
海の波とも映る. 健康な男性諸君に
は, たいていビキニをまとった女性
の胸元に見えるだろう.
(C) : B.J. Designs

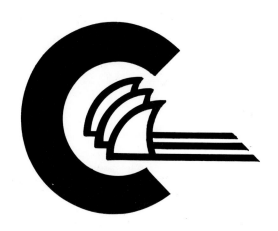

CLUB MALIBU

MALIBU BEACH CLUB

Malibu Beach Club
Retail Clothing Store
A clothing store in America's
most famous beach town. The
accepted logo on the right
looks like sunglasses to some
and ocean waves to others.
Healthy males usually see a
woman's bikini-clad breasts.
Client: B.J. Designs

World Sitizens
Album Cover Title Treatment
Client: Manhattan Records
Art Director: Paula Shear

World Sitizens
レコードジャケットのタイトルデザ
イン
（C）: Manhattan Records
（AD）: Paula Shear

Morgan
My One Year Old Daughter
I decided it was time for her
first logo.
Client: Morgan Nahas Vigon

Morgan
1歳になる愛娘の名前
彼女のために最初のロゴを作っても
いい頃だと思った．
（C）: Morgan Nahas Vigon

Margo Z. Nahas
Illustrator
This logo is for my wife's
company.
Client: Margo Z. Nahas

Margo Z. Nahas
イラストレーターの名前
このロゴは，私の妻の会社用．
（C）: Margo Z. Nahas

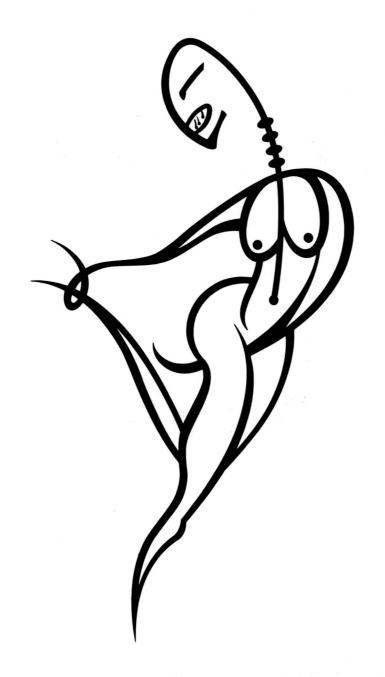

Fertility Goddess
Promotional Logo
An image designed for our self
promotion that proclaimed
our prolificity.
Client: Vigon Seireeni

Fertility Goddess
プロモーション用ロゴ
私達の作品の多産性を宣言するイメ
ージで，自社のプロモーションのた
めデザインした。
（C）: Vigon Seireeni

Couchois
レコードのタイトルデザイン
アートディレクターの話では，バン
ドの連中は何か豹を付したものを希
望しているとのことだった．バンド
の面々にはなぜか会わなかった．最
後には，立体的な刺青模様のような
作風になった．
(C)：Warner Bros. Records
(AD)：John Cabalka
(I)：Margo Z. Nahas

Couchois
Album Title Treatment
The art director said the band
wanted something with a
leopard. Because I never met
the band, I never knew why.
It ended up taking on a three
dimensional tattoo look.
Client: Warner Bros. Records
Art Director: John Cabalka
Illustrator: Margo Z. Nahas

Bon Appetit Article Heads
グルメのための雑誌，"Bon Appetit"
に連載される記事の見出しとしてデ
ザインしたもの．記事の概要を示す
ように，カリグラフィックなタイト
ルのどれにも，字のはねを巧みに利
用して各テーマの内容を図化した絵
が入っている．
（C）: Bon Appetit Magazine
（AD）: Bernie Rotundo & Phillip
Kaplan

Wine Press

New Naturals

Diner's Dictionary

Bon Appetit Article Heads
These were designs for permanent article heads for the gourmet food magazine, Bon Appetit. Each of the calligraphic titles were illustrated with swashes that represented the general theme of the article.
Client: Bon Appetit Magazine
Art Directors: Bernie Rotundo
    & Phillip Kaplan

Sammy Hagar, VOA
Recording Artist & Album Title
    Treatment
Sammy Hagar is the infamous
Red Rocker, last of the solo
guitar/vocalists. The pro-
American theme was partially
inspired by the take-over of
the U.S. Embassy in Teheran.
VOA stands for ''Voice of
America.''
Client: Geffen Records
Illustrator: Margo Z. Nahas

Sammy Hagar, VOA
アーティスト名とそのレコードタイ
トル
Sammy Hager は悪名高い，"レッド
ロッカー"で，リードギター／ヴォ
ーカリストの最後のひとりである．
アメリカびいきのテーマは，テヘラ
ンのアメリカ大使館接収事件からヒ
ントを得た．VOA は，"Voice of
America"（アメリカの声）の略であ
る．
（C）: Geffen Records
（I）: Margo Z. Nahas

**Tom Petty and the
　Heartbreakers**
Recording Group
This was originally designed
for the debut album and con-
tinued to appear on later covers. Tom's famous guitar and
the heart were the obvious
anchors of this design.
Client: Shelter Records

**Tom Petty and the
　Heartbreakers**
アーティスト名
もともとは，グループのデビューア
ルバム用にデザインしたものだが，
ひき続きその後のジャケットにも見
られる．有名な Tom のギターとハ
ートのマークが文字どおりこのデザ
インを支える軸になっている．
(C) : Shelter Records

**Have Yourself A Very Metal
     Christmas**
Christmas Card
This type was developed for a
heavy metal band's Christmas
card.
Client: Quiet Riot

**Have Yourself A Very Metal
     Christmas**
クリスマスカード
ヘビーメタルバンドのクリスマスカ
ードのために考案されたものである.
（C）: Quiet Riot

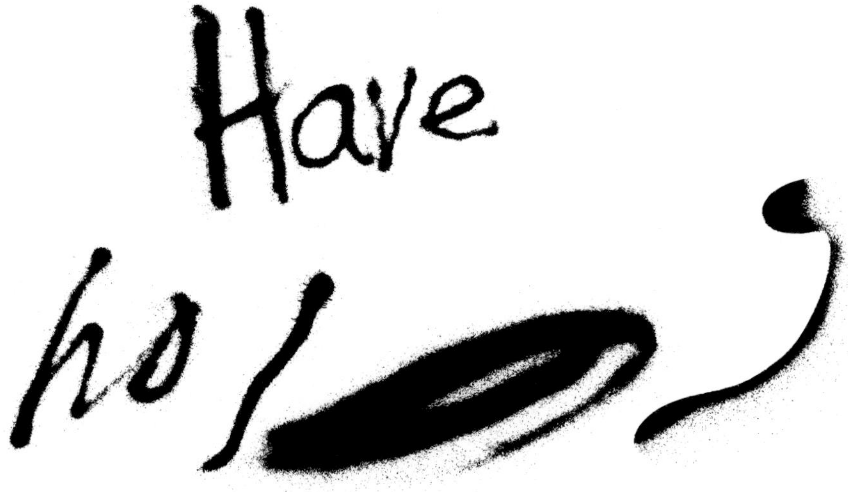

Have yourself
a very Metal
Christmas

Have
ho

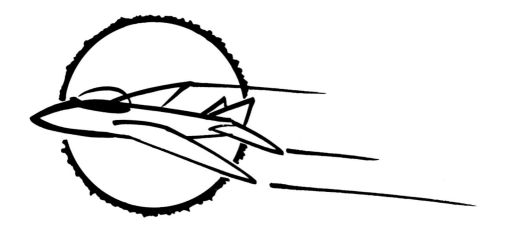

**Kim Carnes, Barking at
  Airplanes**
Album Title Treatment
A dog barking at an airplane.
Get it?
Client: EMI Records
Art Director: Henry Marquez

**Kim Carnes, Barking at
  Airplanes**
レコードのタイトルデザイン
飛行機に向って吠える犬，おわかり
かな？
（C）：EMI Records
（AD）：Henry Marquez

DNA
Album Title Treatment
Two old-time rock 'n rollers
got together to form a new
band. They wanted some-
thing futuristic. I gave them
a molecular model.
Client: Boardwalk Records
Illustrator: Margo Z. Nahas

DNA
レコードのタイトルデザイン
ベテランの2組のロックンローラー
が集って新しいバンドを結成した.
彼らは何か未来感覚のものがいいと
言い，私は分子モデルを彼らに提供
した.
(C)：Broadwalk Records
(I)：Margo Z. Nahas

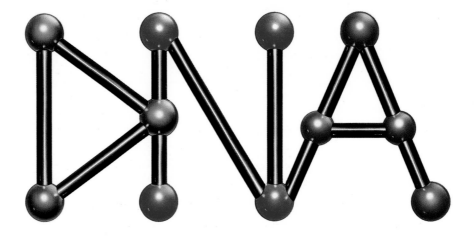

Hughes Thrall
Album Title Treatment
Margo and I decided to make this one look like brass because we were tired of chrome.
Client: CBS Records
Art Director: Tony Lane
Illustrator: Margo Z. Nahas

Hughes Thrall
レコードのタイトルデザイン
クロムにはあきたので，Margo と私は，今度の作品は真鍮仕上げにしようと決めた．
(C)：CBS Records
(AD)：Tony Lane
(I)：Margo Z. Nahas

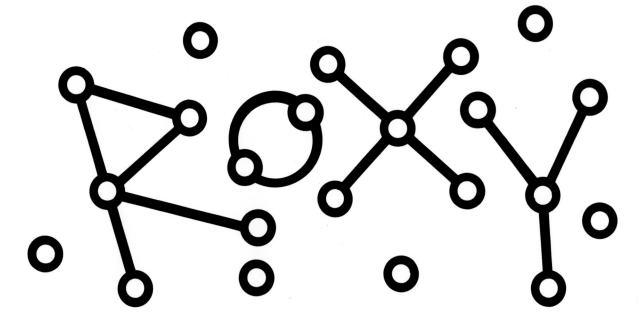

Roxy
洋服の小売店
カリフォルニア北部にある現代風な
洋服店のため，多くのロゴのサンプ
ルを提供した．製作の進行が半分の
ところまできて，クライアントが店
名を "Sodas" に変えてしまったのだ
が，幸いにも，もとの名に戻すこと
になった．
(C)：L.A. Design

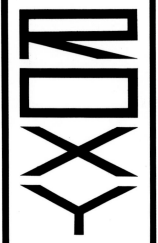

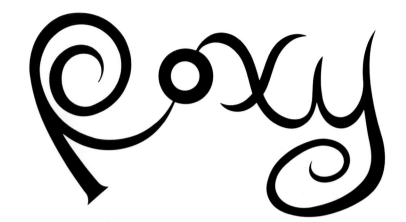

Roxy
Retail Clothing Store
A sampling of many logos presented for a contemporary
clothing store in Northern California. Half way through the
development process, the client changed the name of the
store to "Sodas." Luckily, he
changed it back.
Client: L.A. Design

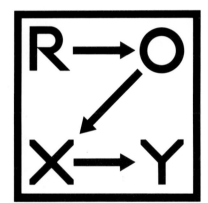

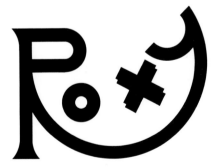

Twenty Twenty
Holiday Health Spa Twentieth
    Anniversary Convention
The client was looking for
something flashy.
Client: J. Walter Thompson
Art Director: Kathy Kosai

Twenty Twenty
ヘルススパの20周年記念コンベン
ション
クライアントは派手めな感じのもの
を期待していた.
（C）: J. Walter Thompson
（AD）: Kathy Kosai

Motown Limited Edition
Special Record Series Logo
The client had requested a
logo to distinguish a special
re-release of classic Motown
albums. The wax seal was
a nice departure from the
chrome lettering so preva-
lent in album cover design
at that time.
Client: Motown Records
Art Director: John Cabalka
Illustrator: Margo Z. Nahas

Motown Limited Edition
特別版レコードのシリーズロゴ
クライアントは，クラッシックな
Motownレコードの再リリースとい
う点を際立たせるようなロゴを求め
てきた．封ろうを用いた事で，当時
のレコードジャケットのデザインで
かなり流行ったクロム・レタリング
からうまく差別化されたわけである．
（C）: Motown Records
（AD）: John Cabalka
（I）: Margo Z. Nahas

Rag Stag Night
Charity Fund Raising Event
This was a black-tie, fund
raising event with proceeds
going to needy workers in the
garment business. The affair
was for men only.
Client: Neil Breton
Art Director: Amy Greenberg

Rag Stag Night
チャリティイベント
衣料関係者が困っている人たちのた
めに開催した資金調達のためのチャ
リティイベント．ブラックタイ着用
のフォーマルな会で，男性のみが参
加した．
（C）：Neil Breton
（AD）：Amy Greenberg

Robert Bane
Art Publisher
The client had seen
another ribbon logo that
I had designed and liked it
so much that he requested
one for himself.
Client: Robert Bane Publishing

Robert Bane
美術出版社
クライアントは私がかってデザイン
した別のリボンのロゴを見たことが
あり，それを大変気に入っていたら
しい．それで今回彼自身も一点注文
することになった．
（C）：Robert Bane Publishing

The Bzz
Album Title Treatment
Another logo done in the hey-
day of chrome lettering. I tried
to make the logo look like a
barbed stinger.
Client: CBS Records
Art Director: Nancy Donald
Illustrator: Margo Z. Nahas

The Bzz
レコードのタイトルデザイン
クロム・レタリングの全盛期に作ら
れたロゴ. ロゴが針のように見える
よう試みた.
(C) : CBS Records
(AD) : Nancy Donald
(I) : Margo Z. Nahas

Fiesta
Charity Ball
Client: Child Help U.S.A.

Fiesta
チャリティ・ダンスパーティー
（C）: Child Help U.S.A.

Righteous Apples
Television Series
Client: Topper Carew

Righteous Apples
テレビ番組のシリーズ
（C）: Topper Carew

Strokes of Genius
Television Series
Client: KCET

Strokes of Genius
テレビ番組のシリーズ
（C）: KCET

Studio 1201
婦人服の会社
クライアントは若い層にアピールするような，どこか違いのあるものを要望した．結局彼らが選んだのはどちらかといえば保守的な作品だったので，たぶん私のデザインでは極短すぎると受けとられたのだろうと思う．
（C）: Mercedes and Adrienne

STUDIO
1201

Studio 1201
Women's Clothing Company
The client requested something different that would appeal to a young audience. Perhaps I went overboard, because the one they chose was rather conservative. It is not shown here.
Client: Mercedes and Adrienne

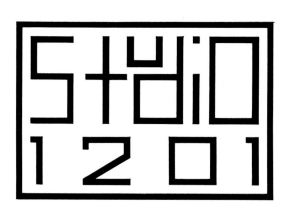

Studio
1201

Studio
1201

Twelve-O-One

Max Studio
婦人服の会社
この解釈にあたり私が心に留めてい
たのは，デザイナーがシーズン毎に
取り組まねばならない流行のスタイ
ルや影響を手品師のごとく扱うとい
うその本能を表現することであった．
Max Studio のタイプはいろいろと
異なる形でも使えよう．この企画向
けの下絵がこのページに示してある．
（C）: Leon Max

Max Studio
Women's Clothing Company
What I had in mind with
this solution was the
skill involved in juggling the
influences and trends that a
designer must cope with every
season. The Max Studio type
can also be used separately in
several different configurations.
The preliminary sketches for
this project are shown on
the left.
Client: Leon Max

Ñusta
綿のスポーツウェア輸入業者
ペルー綿のスポーツウェア専門の新
進企業. クライアントがこれを見て
とてもペルー調だと言ってくれたが,
お世辞かもしれない.
(C) : Cristina Ostoja

ÑUSTA

PURE COTTON FROM PERU

Ñusta
Cotton Sportswear Importer
A new company specializing
in cotton sportswear from
Peru. I took it as a compliment
when the client said it looked
very Peruvian.
Client: Cristina Ostoja

Saratoga
Men's Clothing Company
Various eagle heads developed
for a clothing line with an
Americana theme.
Client: Robert Peritz

Saratoga
紳士服の会社
服のブランドにあわせ，アメリカを
意識し，製作したさまざまな鷲のヘ
ッド.
（C）: Robert Peritz

W.A.S.P.
Recording Group Merchandise
    Logo
W.A.S.P. is one of the most
notorious heavy metal bands.
Their covers were shown as
evidence of social decay at
Senate committee hearings
in Washington, D.C.
Client: Capitol Records Inc.
Art Director: Roy Kohara

W.A.S.P.
アーティストの広告宣伝用ロゴ
W.A.S.P.は，最も有名なヘビーメタ
ルバンドである．彼らのレコードジ
ャケットはワシントン D.C.の上院
議員の審問で，社会の腐敗を示す証
拠として提示されたほどである．
（C）: Capitol Records Inc.
（AD）: Roy Kohara

World Sitizens
アーティスト名
このバンドは2人の白人の青年と2
人の黒人青年から構成されている．
バンドのロゴとして表裏のあるコイ
ンをデザインしたのはこれが初めて
である．表側はバンドのメンバーを
表わすよう，縦横線で4分されてお
り，裏側には彼らに共通のヴィジョ
ンを象徴する目が記されている．
(C)：Manhattan Records
(AD)：Paula Shear

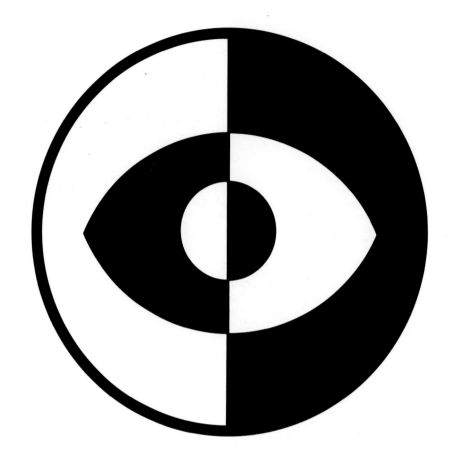

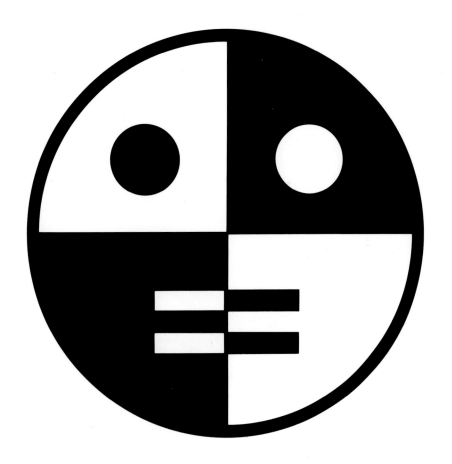

World Sitizens
Recording Group
This band consisted of two
white guys and two black
guys. This is the first band
logo that I designed like a coin
with a front and back. The
face side is quartered to represent the band members, and
on the back is an eye that represents their common vision.
Client: Manhattan Records
Art Director: Paula Shear

L.T.D.
Album Title Treatment
Client: A&M Records
Art Director: Chuck Beeson

L.T.D.
レコードのタイトルデザイン
（C）: A&M Records
（AD）: Chuck Beeson

A.H. Racing
Exotic Car Importer
Client: Evros Stakis

A.H. Racing
外車の輸入業者
（C）: Evros Stakis

Laso
Album Title Treatment
Client: MCA Records
Art Director: George Osaki

Laso
レコードのタイトルデザイン
（C）: MCA Records
（AD）: George Osaki

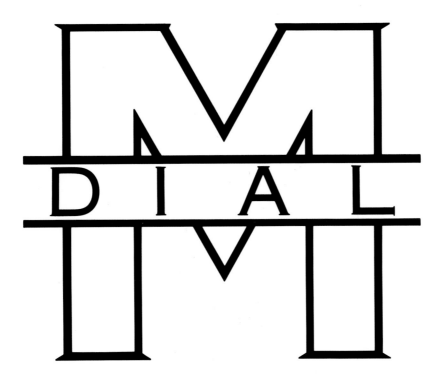

Dial M
Recording Group
The cover design had a sur-
real, DaDa quality, so I looked
to the German type designers
of the 20's for influence.
Client: D&D Records

Dial M
アーティスト名
レコードジャケットのデザインが，
シュールレアリズム，ダダイズムの
特性を備えたものだったので，20年
代のドイツの典型的デザイナーにそ
の影響を探ってみた．
（C）: D&D Records

Dear Mom,
Mattel Toys Trade Ad
I asked my wife to write it with her left hand.
Client: Ogilvy & Mather
Art Director: Shawn Kelly

Dear Mom,
玩具貿易会社の広告
私は妻にこれを左手で書いてくれるよう頼んだ。
(C) : Ogilvy & Mather
(AD) : Shawn Kelly

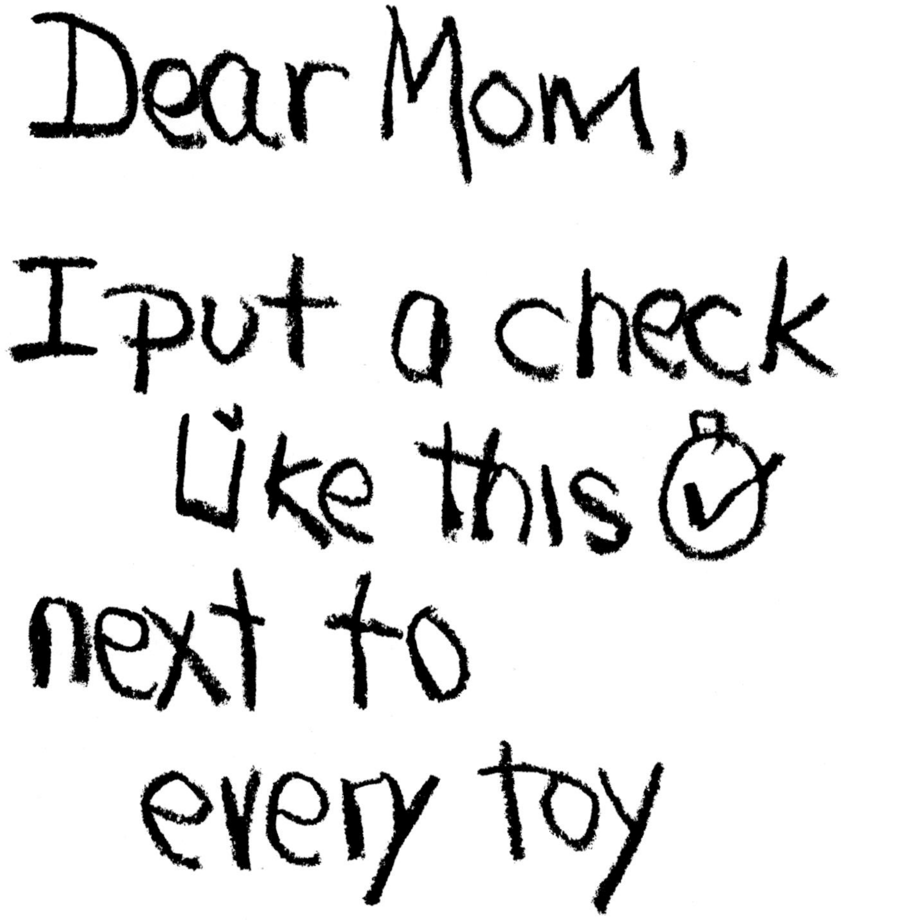
Dear Mom,
I put a check
like this
next to
every toy
I like.
Love, Me

Ain't No Flies In Heaven
'Cause The Back Do' Shut
Stage Play
The backdrop of this play was
a prison setting. The actors
involved the audience to such
an extent that they actually
felt like prisoners.
Client: Vic Bulluck

**Ain't No Flies In Heaven
'Cause The Back Do' Shut**
演劇
この芝居の背景は刑務所．舞台上の
セットもそれに合わせてあり，観客
は俳優達により，実際に自らも囚人
になったと錯覚するほどまで芝居に
巻きこまれていく．
（C）：Vic Bulluck

YUM
CHA
DIM
SUM

Yum Cha
東洋風の軽食レストランチェーン
"Yum Cha"（飲茶）とは、「友人と
お茶を飲む」ことである。この企画
でロゴを考案するにあたり、私は
数々の異なるタイプの中国風モチー
フを調べた。初回に提出したデザイ
ンのうち、私は特に右にあるドラゴ
ンが気に入っていた。
（C）：L.A.Design

Yum Cha
Oriental Fast Food
    Restaurant Chain
The meaning of Yum Cha is
"Having Tea with Friends."
In developing a logo for this
project, I explored many,
many different Chinese motifs.
Of the designs submitted at
the first presentation, I par-
ticularly liked the dragon
on the right.
Client: L.A. Design

Yum Cha
東洋風の軽食レストランチェーン
クライアントとの2度目の打ち合わ
せでは，満足気な表情の猫のデザイ
ンがかなり気に入ってもらえた．し
かしながら，これを満足気な人物に
した場合のグラフィック的に可能な
ところまでさらにやってみてほしい
との注文がでてしまった．
(C)：L.A. Design

Yum Cha
Oriental Fast Food
   Restaurant Chain
During our second round of
presentations to this client,
the representation of a con-
tented cat found much favor.
However, there was an addi-
tional request to explore the
graphic possibilities of a con-
tented human character.
Client: L.A. Design

Yum Cha
東洋風の軽食レストランチェーン
種々の予備スケッチ.
(C) : L.A. Design

Yum Cha
Oriental Fast Food
  Restaurant Chain
Various preliminary sketches.
Client: L.A. Design

Yum Cha
東洋風の軽食レストランチェーン
左側にあるキャラクターが3度目に
提示されたもので,食べ物を持って
満足気な客の姿を表わしている.人
物は可愛いのだが,中国人の漫画
化には賛否両論あるのではないかと
いう心配があった.最終的に受け入
れられたロゴは右ページのものであ
った.おもしろいことに,このモチ
ーフは,最初に提示した分の一部で,
その時にはあまりに単純すぎると思
われたものだった.
(C):L.A.Design

Yum Cha
Oriental Fast Food
    Restaurant Chain
The characters on the left
made up the third presentation and represented a con-
tented customer with his food
to-go. Although the character
was cute, there was a fear that
a Chinese caricature might be
controversial. The logo that
was finally approved is on the
right. It's interesting to note
that this motif was part of the
original presentation and was
thought to be too simple at
that time.
Client: L.A. Design

P.O.V.
スポーツウェアのブランドマーク
スポーツウェアの会社が, ある特殊
な市場での売り上げを促進するため
に, 子会社 (副産部門) を作るのは
よくあることだ. 彼らはロゴやブラ
ンド・アイデンティティの件のみな
らず, 社名を求めてよく私達の所へ
やってくる. Saratoga は, 新種のサ
ービス業界で働く若手のスペシャリ
ストを対象にした分野で開発を進め
てきた. このグループが追求する服
は, 仕事や夜の外出に着ても十分ド
レッシィで, しかもなお週末の遊び
着としても通用するカジュアルなも
のであった. シリコンバレー・ルッ
ク──P.O.V. は, カメラマンの言う
P.O.V. つまり視点のことであり, 若
いビジネスマン向けの服を見つめる
新たな方法を示唆している.
（C）: Bill Kapler

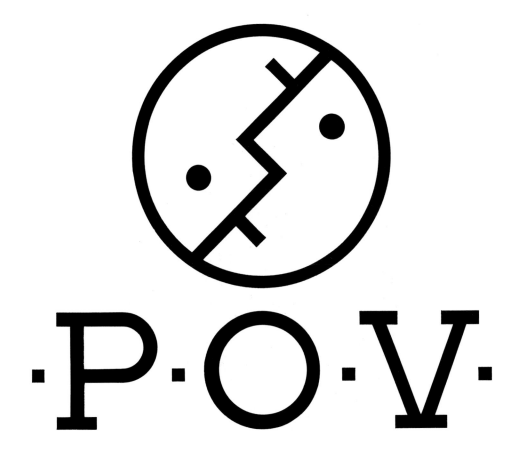

P.O.V.
Division of Saratoga
    Sportswear
It's a frequent practice for
sportswear companies to create spin-off lines to promote
sales in certain specialized
markets. Often they come to
us for the name as well as the
logo and identity program.
Saratoga had developed a line
aimed at young professionals
in the new service industries.
This group wanted clothes
that were dressy enough for
work and evening, yet casual
enough for weekends. The
silicon valley look. P.O.V. is a
cameraman's term for Point of
View and suggested a new way
of looking at wardrobes for
young businessmen.
Client: Bill Kapler

I.N.P.C.
出版社
会社自体は新しいのだが，彼らはか
なり歴史があり広く経験をもつ会社
に見せるようなロゴを希望していた．
(C)：I.N.P.C.

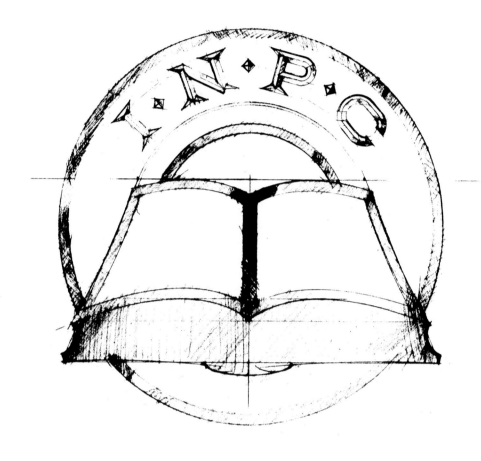

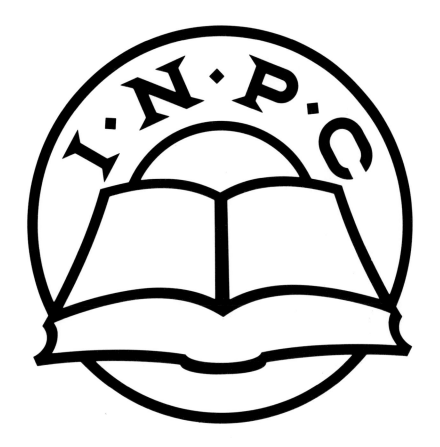

I.N.P.C.
Publishing Company
This was a new publishing
company, but they wanted a
logo which made them appear
as though they had been
around for a hundred years.
Client: I.N.P.C.

The Splat Brothers
Design Firm
Another rejected logo devel-
oped for The Fabulous Picasso
Bros. that we ultimately used
for our own promotion.
Client: Vigon Seireeni

The Splat Brothers
デザイン会社
Fabulous Picasso Bros.のために製
作したが不採用になり，最終的には
自社のプロモーションのために使っ
た．
（C）：Vigon Seireeni

Dueling Artists
Design Firm
Another self promotion logo
used on note pads, rubber
stamps, etc.
Client: Vigon Seireeni

Dueling Artists
デザイン会社
自社のメモ用箋やゴム印他に使用し
たプロモーションロゴ.
（C）: Vigon Seireeni

ESTA
音楽出版・レコード会社
クライアントは何か独特な感じを求
めており，ESTA という言葉には特
別な意味がこめられていなかったた
め，私は特異な感じがする文字にし
ようと思った．
（C）: Evros Stakis

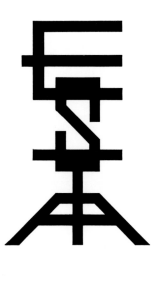

ESTA
Music Publishing & Recording
  Company
The client wanted something
different, and because the
word did not mean anything
in particular, I explored some
off-the-wall letter forms.
Client: Evros Stakis

David Lee Roth
 Crazy From The Heat
Recording Artist and
 Album Title
Dave is the most colorful
client that we've ever worked
with and certainly the most
flamboyant. As the front man
for Van Halen, he earned the
reputation as the clown prince
of rock and roll. I think I cap-
tured his spirit with this logo.
I only had one day to come up
with a solution because Dave
was leaving for an expedition
to Head Hunter territory in
New Guinea.
Client: Diamond Dave
Enterprises

David Lee Roth
 Crazy From The Heat
アーティスト名とレコードタイトル
Dave はこれまで一緒に仕事をした
中で最も生彩があって，しかもまち
がいなく一番クレージーだ．Van
Halen の看板男として，ロックンロ
ールの道化の王との異名を取ってい
る．私はこのロゴで彼の心意気をと
らえられたと思う．Dave がニュー
ギニアの首狩り族の領地へ探検の旅
に出てしまうというので，仕上げる
までたった一日しかなかった．
（C）：Diamond Dave Enterprises

Crazy From The Heat
    The Movie
Movie Title Treatment
This movie was a spin off from
the record project. The logo
on the left would have been
perfectly adequate, but, true
to form, the movie company
wanted a logo that tried to
explain the entire contents of
the film…tropical paradise,
women and rock 'n roll. One
of many rejected designs.
Client: CBS Productions

Crazy From The Heat
    The Movie
映画のタイトル・デザイン
この映画はレコードの企画からの副
産物である。左にあるロゴは本当に
うってつけのものだったが、映画会
社側は型通りに、映画の内容すべて
を説明し得るようなロゴを求めてき
た。つまり…トロピカル、楽園、女、
ロックンロールといったもの。不採
用になったうちのひとつ。
(C)：CBS Productions

Hello
Letterhead Design
Client: Vigon Nahas Vigon

Hello
レターヘッドのデザイン
(C)：Vigon Nahas Vigon

California
Mail Order Gift Catalog
Client: California

California
通信販売のギフトカタログ
(C)：California

Knable
Artist Representative
Client: Ellen Knable & Assoc.

Knable
アーティストのレップ（マネージャー）
(C)：Ellen Knable & Assoc.

Child Help U.S.A.
Charity Organization's
	Twenty-Fifth Anniversary
The client had requested a
classic design incorporating
their dove logo.
Client: Child Help U.S.A.

Child Help U.S.A.
慈善団体の25周年記念
クライアントは，彼らのシンボルで
ある鳩のロゴを組み入れた，クラッ
シックなデザインを求めた．
(C)：Child Help U.S.A.

Tropicana
Hotel and Entertainment
    Complex
This was a design for the
famous Las Vegas landmark.
Client: Doyle Dane Bernbach,
    West
Art Director: Mel Sant

Tropicana
ホテルと娯楽施設
有名なラスベガスの名所のデザイン.
(C)：Doyle Dane Bernbach, West
(AD)：Mel Sant

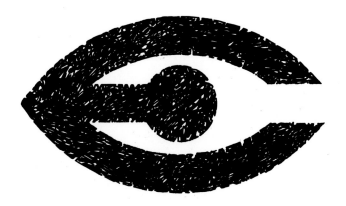

E·R·S· GALLERY

E.R.S. Gallery
Russian Avant Garde Art
   Gallery
Client: Evros Stakis

E.R.S. Gallery
ロシアのアバン・ギャルド派のアー
ト・ギャラリー
(C)：Evros Stakis

SHOUT DEVO

Shout Devo
Album Title Treatment
Client: Warner Bros. Records

Shout Devo
レコードのタイトル・デザイン
(C): Warner Bros. Records

Insane
Recording Company
Client: Insane Records

Insane
レコード会社
(C): Insane Records

The Quick
Album Title Treatment
Client: Desmond Stroble

The Quick
レコードのタイトル・デザイン
(C): Desmond Stroble

Fatigue
Fragrance Packaging Logo
Client: Camp Beverly Hills

Fatigue
香水のパッケージ用ロゴ
(C)：Camp Beverly Hills

Dain & DeJoy
Recording Company
Client: Buddy Dane &
　　　Ed DeJoy

Dain & DeJoy
レコード会社
(C)：Buddy Dane & Ed DeJoy

Tusk Tour
Recording Group Tour Logo
Client: Penguin Productions

Tusk Tour
レコーディング・アーティストのツ
アー公演用ロゴ
(C)：Penguin Productions

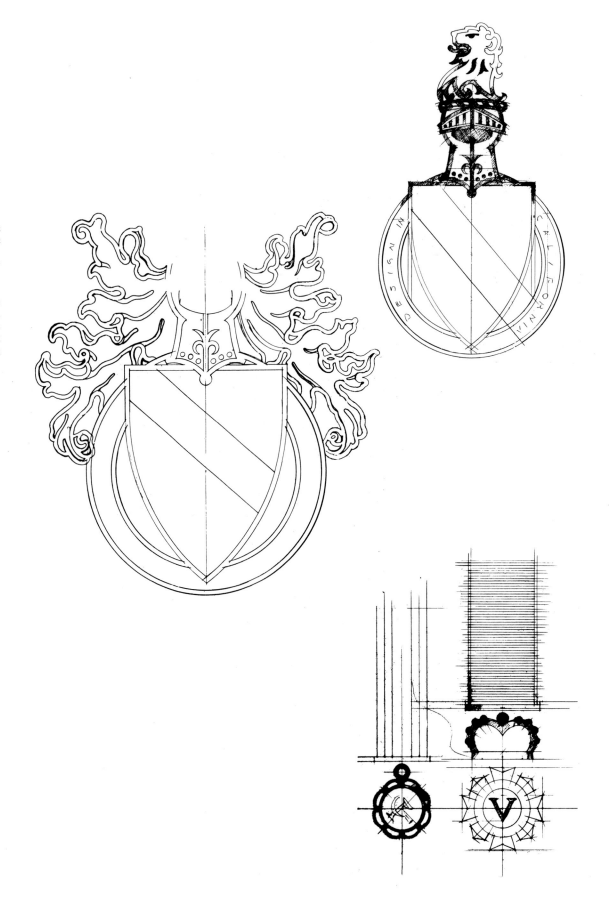

**Armorial Bearings of
Sir Vigon Seireeni**

彼の地位に利をもたらすような東洋
風のかぶとの上方，リボンに黒文字
で "Vigon Seireeni" と記され，ライ
オンの半像が乗っている．盾形の下
には "Design in California" という
モットーが配され，その功労に対し
授与されたメダルが赤と緑のしまの
飾りひもに付き，３ヶ所に下げられ
ている．盾の中には，対角線上に小
型の３頭のグリフィンが配され，不
気味な頭蓋骨と，鉛筆を押す男の像
があしらわれている．

(C)：Vigon Seireeni

Armorial Bearings of Sir Vigon Seireeni
Over an Eastern helmet befitting his degree, the ribbon inscribed "Vigon Seireeni" in letters sable and a demi-lion rampant. Below the escutcheon charged with the motto, "Design in California" three pendants from a riband tenné, medals conferred upon for service alternately gules and vert. In the argent, three demi-griffins charged with a lozenge in bend of the first, a spiked and sinister headscull and a man pushing a pencil. Client: Vigon Seireeni

Leon Max
Women's Clothing Company
This logo was created for the
cover of one of Leon Max's
catalogs. The catalog had a
"Breakfast at Tiffany's" feeling. I wanted the logo to have
a personal touch, as though it
were written as a note.
Client: Leon Max

Leon Max
婦人服の会社
このロゴは Leon Max 社のカタログ
の表紙用に作られたものである．こ
のカタログは"Breakfast at Tiffany's"
（ティファニーで朝食を）の雰囲気を
もっていた．これは覚え書きのよう
に書かれており，私としては人の何
気ない筆致をもつロゴにしたかった.
(C)：Leon Max

Brand–X
Women's Clothing Company
This logo was also developed
for Leon Max, but for a lower
cost, more youthful line.
Unfortunately, a title search
revealed that another company already had rights to
the name.
Client: Leon Max

Brand–X
婦人服の会社
これも Leon Max 社用に考案された
ロゴだが，より安価で若者向けの路
線の服用．残念なことに，登記をし
ようとしたら，他の会社がすでにこ
の名に対し権利を有していることが
わかってしまった．
(C)：Leon Max

Flavor of the Month
Baskin and Robbins Promotion
Client: J. Walter Thompson
Art Director: Frank Frasier

Flavor of the Month
Baskin and Robbins（アイスクリームの販売促進用）
(C)：J. Walter Thompson
(AD)：Frank Frasier

Runner
Recording Group
Client: Warner Bros. Records
Art Director: John Cabalka

Runner
レコーディング・アーティスト名
(C)：Warner Bros. Records
(AD)：John Cabalka

The Cars Heartbeat Tour
Recording Group Tour Logo
Client: Lookout Management

The Cars Heartbeat Tour
レコーディング・アーティストのツアー公演用ロゴ
(C)：Lookout Managent

Don't Drink and Drive
Public Service Message
Client: Gotcha Sportswear

Don't Drink and Drive
公共事業の標語
(C)：Gotcha Sportswear

Knable
Artist Representative
Client: Ellen Knable & Assoc.

Knable
アーティストのレップ名
(C)：Ellen Knable & Assoc.

Dave T.V.
Music Video Prop
Client: Diamond Dave
    Enterprises

Dave T.V.
音楽ビデオの舞台セット
(C)：Diamond Dave Enterprises

Sutseso
Couture Clothing Company
The image was designed to
support an advertising theme
based on Darwin's Theory of
Natural Selection. The designer's clothes were a hybrid of
style influenced by the best
couture designs of the last
four decades.
Client: World Company Ltd.
Art Director: Yoshiaki Nakano

Sutseso
高級婦人服の会社
このイメージは，ダーウィンの自然
淘汰論を基にした広告のテーマを支
えるように，デザインされたもので
ある．デザイナーの造る服は，過去
40年で最も素晴しい仕立てのデザイ
ンに影響を受けたスタイルをいろい
ろと取り混ぜた形式のものであった．
(C)：World Company Ltd.
(AD)：Yoshiaki Nakano

sú"tʃeso

CREATIVE PLANET

Creative Planet
Artist Resource Company
The mixing of different animal
parts suggested the creation
of one animal with the talents
of many. Creative Planet was
designed to bring various
artists together to work on
common projects.
Client: Yoshiaki Nakano &
Shi Yu Chen

Creative Planet
アーティストの人材派遣会社
異なる動物の身体の部分を結合させ
ることで，多くの才能もつ１つの動
物を創造することを暗示している．
Creative Planet は，共通の企画で
様々なアーティストが一緒に働くよ
うにするため計画された．
(C)：Yoshiaki Nakano & Shi Yu Chen

Lyons & Clark
Album Title Treatment
Client: Shelter Records

Lyons & Clark
レコードのタイトル・デザイン
(C)：Shelter Records

Carpenters
Album Title Treatment
Client: A&M Records
Art Director: Chuck Beeson

Carpenters
レコードのタイトル・デザイン
(C)：A & M Records
（AD）：Chuck Beeson

The Four Seasons, Story
Album Title Treatment
Client: Rick Rogers

The Four Seasons, Story
レコードのタイトル・デザイン
(C)：Rick Rogers

Together
Album Title Treatment
Client: RCA Records

Together
レコードのタイトル・デザイン
(C)：RCA Records

Feels So Good
Album Title Treatment
The art director said she
wanted the letters to look cozy
'n comfy. It turned out to be a
popular T-shirt.
Client: A&M Records
Art Director: Juni Osaki

Feels So Good
レコードのタイトル・デザイン
アートディレクターは文字がこじん
まりしていて、気分が良くなるよう
なものを希望していた。その結果、
ポピュラーなTシャツになった。
(C)：A & M Records
(AD)：Juni Osaki

Undercover Wear
婦人用肌着の通信販売会社
左上の二点のロゴは女性をほのめか
す花のモチーフである．左下のロゴ
は，製品を着用することからくるロ
マンチックな雰囲気を思わせている．
クライアントは右のロゴでいくこと
に決めた．彼らはただただリボンが
よかったのである．
(C)：Robert Bane Publishing

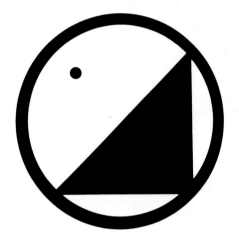

Undercover Wear
Women's Mail-order Lingerie
    Company
The two logos on the top left
are flower motifs suggesting
feminine genitalia. The logo
on the bottom left suggests the
romantic possibilities of wearing the product. They went
with the one on the right. The
client just wanted ribbons.
Client: Robert Bane Publishing

Keiko For Men
紳士用下着の会社
Keiko は私の相棒の旧友で，婦人用
水着のデザイナーとして最も有名で
ある．1984年に，彼女は紳士用下着
を市場に出す企画をおこした．私は
幾つかの候補作をデザインしたが，
右の一点が一番気に入っていた．こ
れは，Karl Schulpig のデザインによ
る1923年のロゴから採用された．
(C)：Tucker International

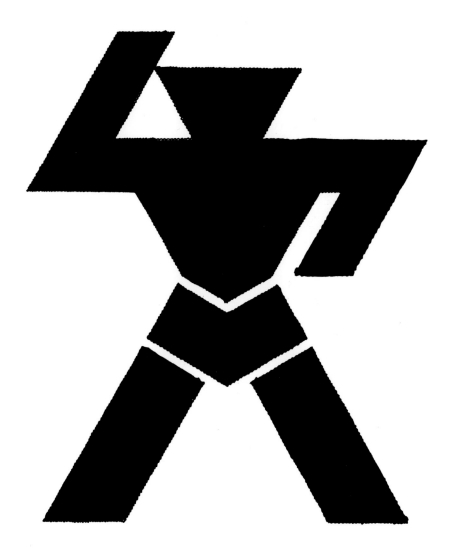

Keiko For Men
Men's Underwear Company
Keiko was an old friend of my
partner. She's best known as a
women's swimwear designer.
In 1984, she organized a project to market men's underwear.
I designed several alternatives,
but I liked the one on the right
best. It was influenced by
a 1923 logo designed by
Karl Schulpig.
Client: Tucker International

The Dramatics
Album Cover Title Treatment
Client: ABC Records
Art Director: Stewart Kusher

The Dramatics
レコードのタイトル・デザイン
(C)：ABC Records
(AD)：Stewart Kusher

Pets, Wet Behind The Ears
Recording Group and
Album Title
Client: A&M Records
Art Director: Juni Osaki

Pets, Wet Behind The Ears
レコーディング・アーティスト名と
レコードのタイトル
(C)：A & M Records
(AD)：Juni Osaki

Virgil
Stage Play
Client: Vic Bulluck

Virgil
演劇
(C)：Vic Bulluck

Barely Legal
Women's Swimwear Company
Client: Barely Legal

Barely Legal
婦人用水着の会社
(C)：Barely Legal

Super Funtastic
Advertising Promotion
Client: P.F.T.
Art Director: Barry
　Sherachefski

Super Funtastic
広告宣伝
(C)：P.F.T.
(AD)：Barry Sherachefski

Sheila
Magazine Article Treatment
Client: Chic Magazine
Art Director: Bill Skursky

Sheila
雑誌の記事の見出しデザイン
(C)：Chic Magazine
(AD)：Bill Skursky'

The Garage
Retail Clothing Store
The Garage was a proposal for
a men's sportswear store. Like
the Malibu Laundry project,
this was another marketing
concept based on logo as product. Their merchandise
included T-shirts, sweats and
other common sportswear
items, and could only be dis-
tinguished from their compet-
itor's product by the logo.
Client: B.J. Designs

The Garage
洋服の小売店
The Garage は, 紳士用スポーツウェ
ア店のため提案されたものであった.
Malibu Laundry 社のプロジェクト
と同様に, これもロゴを商品として
とらえるマーケティングの概念の一
例である. 商品構成は, Tシャツ, ス
ウェット着, その他一般のスポーツ
ウェアで, 競合商品とは, そのロゴ
によって見分けるしかない.
(C)：B.J. Designs

Futura
Recording Company
The logo is a whimsical depiction of the future.
Client: Ron Ellison

Futura
レコード会社
このロゴは，未来を風変わりに描写
している．
(C) : Ron Ellison

Primal Institute
Psychology Institute
Various designs for an
institute that specializes in
"Primal Scream" therapy.
Client: Primal Institute

Primal Institute
心理学研究所
"Primal Scream"療法を専門にして
いる研究所のための様々なデザイン.
(C)：Primal Institute

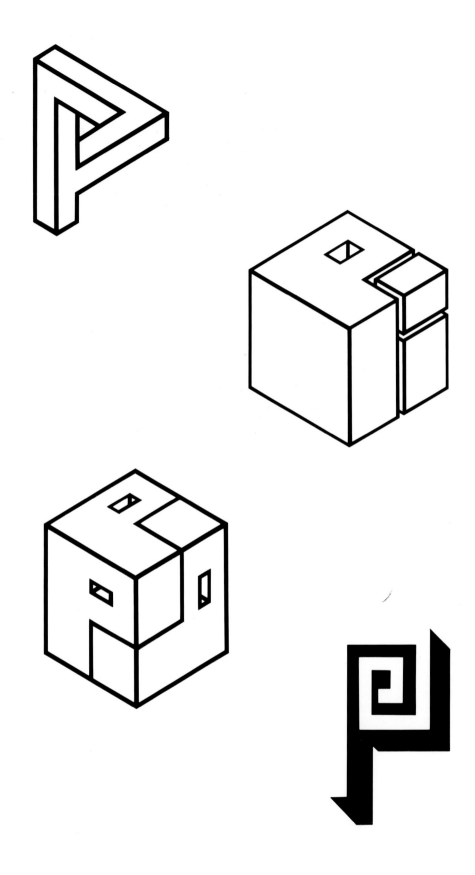

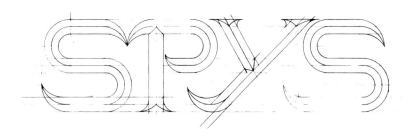

Spys
Album Title Treatment
The band didn't like any
of these, but I thought they
were clever.
Client: EMI Records
Art Director: Bill Burks

Spys
レコードのタイトル・デザイン
バンドの連中はどれもお気に召さな
かったが, 私は器用な出来だと思った.
(C)：EMI Records
（AD）：Bill Burks

Media B
紳士服の会社
いろいろな傾向のものを探究してみ
たあと，我々は服のラインを代表す
るようなキャラクターに集中してと
りかかることに決めた．Hathaway
Shirt 社で有名な Hathaway の顔と
同様に，我々のキャラクターはア
イ・パッチをしている．しかし Media
B のこの男の顔は更に一歩進んで，
ロマンチックなプロ，真実や正義を
シリコンバレー風に求めて地球をさ
まよう調査報道員などの姿をほのめ
かしている．
(C)：Bill Kapler

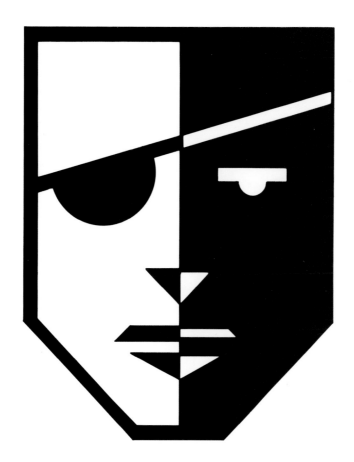

Media B
Men's Clothing Company
After exploring several directions, we decided to concentrate on a character that would represent the clothing line. Like the Hathaway man of Hathaway Shirt fame, our character had an eye patch. But the Media B man went a step further and suggested a romantic professional, an investigative reporter who roamed the earth searching for truth, justice, and the Silicon Valley way.
Client: Bill Kapler

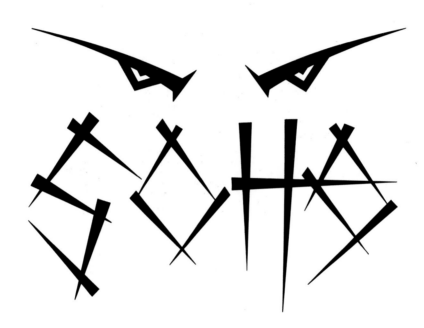

Soho 1984
ナイトクラブ
このクラブの番地が1984番で, 営業
開始が1984年, "Big brother is watching" といったジョージ・オーウェ
ル風なテーマが, スケッチを書く自
然な方向だと思えた. とはいえ, 我々
は右の一点が最も気に入った.
(C)：Soho 1984

Soho 1984
Night Club
The street address of this club was 1984, and it opened for business in 1984. The Orwellian theme of "big brother is watching" seemed like a natural direction for some of the sketches. However, we liked the one on the right best.
Client: Soho 1984

Cole of California
    60th Anniversary
Women's Swimwear Company
Cole is the world's oldest
swimwear company, and on
the anniversary of their 60th
year in business, they held an
event for which this logo was
designed. Despite the obvious
imagery, we discovered that
no other swimwear company
was using a mermaid for
it's logo.
Client: Cole of California
Art Director: Sheri Mobley

Cole of California
    60th Anniversary
婦人用水着の会社
Cole は世界で最も歴史の長い水着
メーカーで，創業60周年にあたり，
記念行事を催した．その際，デザイ
ンされたのがこのロゴであった．す
ぐ見てわかるイメージにもかかわら
ず，どの水着メーカーもロゴに人魚
を使ってはいないことに我々は気が
ついた．
(C)：Cole of California
〔AD〕：Sheri Mobley

Muffin Oven
Fast Food Chain
Client: L.A. Design

Muffin Oven
ファースト・フードのチェーン店
(C)：L.A. Design

Lita Ford
Recording Artist
Client: Polygram Records
Art Director: Bill Levy

Lita Ford
レコーディング・アーティスト名
(C)：Polygram Records
（AD）：Bill Levy

Black 'N Blue
Recording Group Tour Logo
Client: Geffen Records

Black 'N Blue
レコーディング・アーティストの
ツアー公演用ロゴ
(C)：Geffen Records

Quiet Riot
Recording Group
Client: CBS/Pasha Records

Quiet Riot
レコーディング・アーティスト名
(C)：CBS／Pasha Records

George Thorogood, Bad To
  The Bone
Album Title Treatment
I purposely made this logo
look crude, like a home-made
tattoo. Rejected.
Client: EMI Records
Art Director: Bill Burks

George Thorogood, Bad To
  The Bone
レコードのタイトル・デザイン
私はこのロゴを，自製の刺青のよう
に，あえて生硬にみえるようにして
みたが不採用となった.
(C)：EMI Records
(AD)：Bill Burks

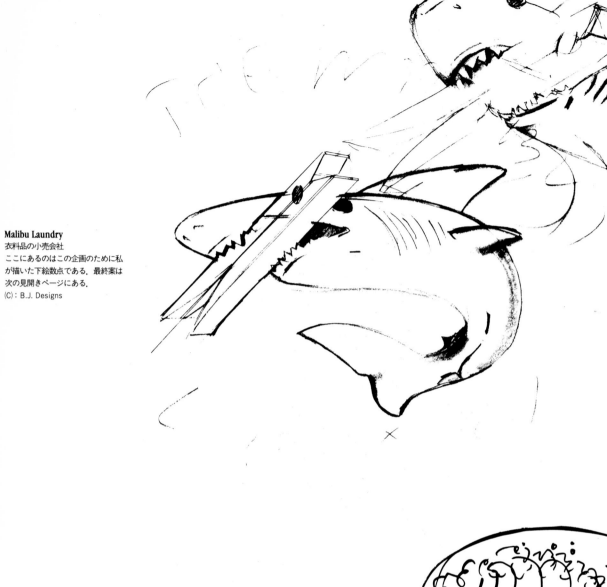

Malibu Laundry
衣料品の小売会社
ここにあるのはこの企画のために私
が描いた下絵数点である. 最終案は
次の見開きページにある.
(C)：B.J. Designs

Malibu Laundry
Retail Clothing Company
These were some of my
preliminary sketches for this
project. The final solutions
are on the following pages.
Client: B.J. Designs

The Malibu Laundry
Retail Clothing Company
These three logos were also
used as supplemental graphics
for Malibu Laundry products.
Client: B.J. Designs

The Malibu Laundry
衣料品の小売会社
この3点のロゴもまた，Malibu
Laundry 社の製品用に補足のグラフ
ィックとして使用された．
(C)：B.J. Designs

The Malibu Laundry
Retail Clothing Company
The Malibu Laundry is a clothing store that deals primarily in casual sportswear for girls aged 8 to 14. They're located in Malibu. This is a case where the logo was the product. All of the merchandise in the store, from T-shirts and sweats to towels and garment bags, was emblazoned with the logo. This was the only aspect that differentiated it from merchandise in other stores.
Client: B.J. Designs

The Malibu Laundry
衣料品の小売会社
Malibu Laundry 社は，そもそも 8
〜14才の女の子向けのカジュアル・
スポーツウェアを扱う衣料品店であ
る．これは，ロゴが製品となる例で
あった．Tシャツやスウェットシャ
ツからタオル，服をいれるバッグま
で店にある全商品がこのロゴで飾ら
れた．他店の商品と差別化する唯一
の点がこのロゴであった．
(C)：B.J. Designs

The Fabulous Picasso Brothers
映画製作会社

会社名のブラザースの部分は，Van
Halen の有名な David Lee Roth と
彼の相棒の Pete Angelus，彼らの指
示するところでは，ピザパイと芸術
を暗示するようなロゴが必要だった
らしいが，こういった趣向が示され
るまで私には理解できなかった．私
としては Picasso 流にやってみた．
(C)：Diamond Dave Enterprises

152

The Fabulous Picasso Brothers
Movie Production Company
The brothers are David Lee
Roth, of Van Halen fame, and
his partner Pete Angelus.
Their instructions called for a
logo that suggested pizza and
fine art, but I didn't know
that until after presenting
these ideas. I went after
Picasso.
Client: Diamond Dave
Enterprises

NEXT

NEXT

Next
コンピュータ製造会社
Steve Jobs は Apple Computer 社の
創始者の一人であった．彼は Apple
をやめ，別のコンピュータ会社を始
めた．Next は文字通り，彼の次の事
業のことである．我々はロゴに対す
る仮のアイディアを提出するように
言われた．右のアラジンのランプ風
なロゴは，彼の新しいメガ・バイト・
コンピュータの有する能力や魅力の
特性を示しているのである．
(C)：Next Inc.
(CD)：Susan Kare

next

NEXT

N&XT

NEXT

next

NEXT

Next
Computer Manufacturing
Company
Steve Jobs was one of the
founders of Apple Computer.
He left Apple to start another
computer company. Next was
literally his next project. We
were asked to submit preliminary ideas for his logo. The
Aladdin's lamp logo on the
right represented the qualities
of power and magic in his new
mega-bite computer.
Client: Next Inc.
Creative Director: Susan Kare

Next
コンピュータ製造会社
左にあるコンピュータのくずれ字は
最初は，明解な手法に思えた．しか
し結果として我々は，とても満足し
た．右にある象は，コンピュータの
記憶量と速さを示すものである．ク
ライアントはユーモアを解せなかっ
た．
(C)：Next Inc.
(CD)：Susan Kare

Next
Computer Manufacturing
    Company
The computer distorted type
on the left page seemed like
an obvious approach at first,
but we were quite happy with
the results. The elephant on
the right represented memory
and speed. I don't think the
client appreciated the humor.
Client: Next Inc.
Creative Director: Susan Kare

Next
コンピュータ製造会社
左にあるデザインの数々は，このコンピュータ会社に我々が示した概念上で基本となったロゴのうち，ごくわずかな例にすぎない．この会社の製品は特に大学生向けに考えられたものなので，これらのアイディアの多くに教育的なモチーフが取り込まれた．Nextの社長である Steve Jobsは右の一点が気に入ったようだったが，これでいくかどうか，印刷時になってもはっきりしなかった．
(C)：Next Inc.
(CD)：Susan Kare

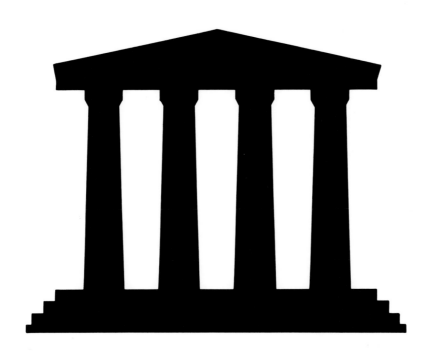

Next
Computer Manufacturing
  Company
The designs on the left
represent just a few of the
conceptually based logos that
we presented to this computer
firm. Since their product is
specifically designed for college students, many of these
ideas involve educational
motifs. Steve Jobs, the presi-
dent of Next, seemed to like
the one on the right, but it
was unclear at press time
whether he would go for it.
Client: Next Inc.
Creative Director: Susan Kare

Pounding Surf
Tシャツのロゴ
このスポーツウェア会社の顧客は常
に新しいTシャツのデザインに飽
くことない興味をもっている。我々
はいつでも新しいデザインのための
アイディアが浮かぶと、それを提出
する。するとクライアントはすぐに
そのデザインを採用するという具合
だ。
(C)：Gotcha Sportswear

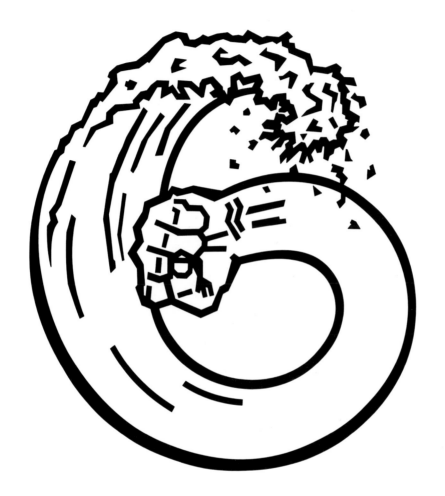

Pounding Surf
T-shirt Logo
This sportswear company's
customers have an insatiable
appetite for new T-shirt
designs. Whenever we get
an idea for a new design,
we send it in, and the client
always uses them.
Client: Gotcha Sportswear

Aloha Paradise
ホリデイ・ヘルス・スパ・ハワイア
ン・コンベンション
フラダンサー，ヤシの木，サーファ
ーといったおきまりのイメージは避
けたかった.
(C)：J. Walter Thompson
（AD）：Wade Davis

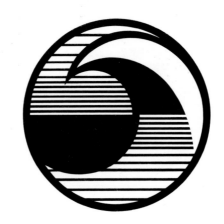

Aloha Paradise
Holiday Health Spa Hawaiian
　Convention
I wanted to avoid cliché
images like hula girls, palm
trees and surfers.
Client: J. Walter Thompson
Art Director: Wade Davis

K.S.N. International
Art Publisher
The client wanted a horse.
Client: K.S.N. International

K.S.N. International
美術系出版業者
クライアントは馬のデザインを希望
していた.
(C)：K.S.N. International

John Butcher, Axis
Recording Artist & Album
  Title Treatment
This piece was partially
inspired by Da Vinci's "Pro-
portions of Man" drawing.
Client: Capitol Records
Art Director: Roy Kohara

John Butcher, Axis
レコーディング・アーティスト名と
レコードのタイトル・デザイン
この作品は，部分的にダヴィンチの
"人体の構図"の絵から着想を得た.
(C)：Capitol Records
（AD）：Roy Kohara

Ellison Productions
Recording Company
Client: Ron Ellison

Ellison Productions
レコード会社
(C)：Ron Ellison

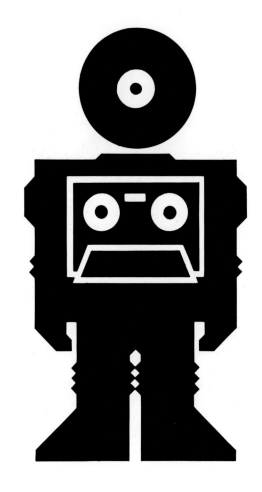

Too Loose To Trek
Clothing Company Catalog
　　Mascot
Client: Camp Beverly Hills

Too Loose To Trek
洋服メーカーのカタログ用マスコット
(C)：Camp Beverly Hills

Table For Five
映画のタイトルデザイン
 3人の子供がいて，離婚した父親に
まつわる映画のため製作された種々
のデザイン例．彼の妻が子供達の保
護者になってはいるが，彼は子供達
を航海に連れ出すことを許される．
航海中，母親が殺されてしまい，劇
的な父権の取り合い合戦を繰りひろ
げ，継父が彼らを追い始める．正に
お涙ちょうだいものである．
（C）: Voight-Schefel

TABLE FOR Five

Table For Five
Movie Title Treatment
These were various treatments
developed for a movie about a
divorced father with three
children. His wife has custody
of the kids, but he's allowed
to take them on a cruise.
While on the boat, the mother
is killed, and the step father
begins chasing after them in a
scenic custody battle. It's a
real tear-jerker.
Client: Voight-Schefel

Tattoo
婦人服会社
これには手こずった。社名から刺青
風の仕上げをしたロゴが浮かんだの
だが、クライアントは刺青模様では
あまりに薄っぺらな感じだととった。
印刷の段になっても、この企画は決
定に至らなかった。
(C)：Breton Industries

Tattoo
Women's Clothing Company
This was a tough one. The
name of the company sug-
gested a logo with tattoo char-
acteristics; however, the client
felt that tattoos were too
sleazy. At press time, this project still hadn't been resolved.
Client: Breton Industries

Bowie, Jagger

レコードのタイトル・デザイン
これらのデザインはもともと，
David Bowie と Mick Jagger による
シングルレコード，"Dancin' In The
Street" のために創られたものであ
る．これらは不採用となったが，
Bowie 版の方はダンス・ミックス用
に再提出された．これもまたその企
画には受け入れられなかった．私と
しては機会さえあれば，もう一度提
出してもいいと思うほど気に入って
いる．

（C）：EMI Records
（AD）：HenryMarquez

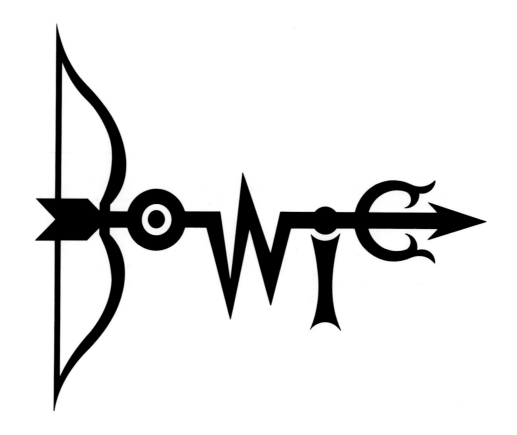

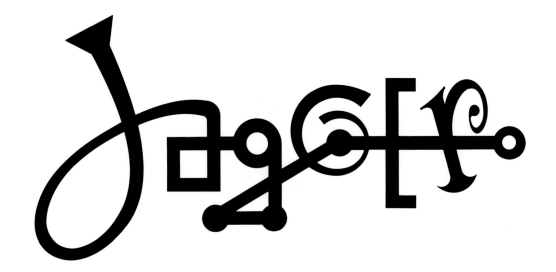

Bowie, Jagger
Album Title Treatment
These designs were originally
created for the single, "Dancin' In The Streets" by David
Bowie and Mick Jagger. They
were rejected, but the Bowie
version was re-submitted for
a dance-mix album. It was
also rejected for that project.
I like it enough to submit it
again if I get the chance.
Client: EMI Records
Art Director: Henry Marquez

Still The Beaver
Television Series Title
Client: Brian LeVant

Still The Beaver
テレビ番組シリーズのタイトル
(C)：Brian LeVant

Gentle Persuasion
Album Title Treatment
Client: Warner Bros. Records
Art Director: Ed Thrasher

Gentle Persuasion
レコードのタイトル・デザイン
(C)：Warner Bros. Records
（AD）：Ed Thrasher

Dangerous
Album Title Treatment
Client: CBS/Pasha Records

Dangerous
レコードのタイトル・デザイン
(C)：CBS／Pasha Records

A Chorus Line
Movie Title Treatment
This movie was adapted from
the famous Broadway musical.
I tried to design something
that was different from the
20's style graphics that were
associated with the stage version and, instead, suggest the
motion of dance.
Client: Ed Thrasher & Assoc.

A Chorus Line
映画のタイトル・デザイン
この映画は有名なブロードウェイ・
ミュージカルを脚色したものである.
私は舞台版を連想させる'20年代の
グラフィックとは違う何かをデザイ
ンしようと試み, 代わりにダンスの
躍動感をほのめかすようにした.
(C): Ed Thrasher & Assoc.

Autograph
Recording Group
Client: RCA Records

Autograph
レコーディング・グループ名
(C)：RCA Records

Heaven
Recording Group
Client: Browning Management

Heaven
レコーディング・グループ名
(C)：Browning Management

Revolt In The Stars
Movie Title Treatment
Client: P.F.T.

Revolt In The Stars
映画のタイトル・デザイン
(C)：P.F.T.

Sammy Hagar, V.O.A.
Recording Artist and Album
   Title Treatment
Client: Geffen Records

Sammy Hagar, V.O.A.
レコーディング・アーティスト名と
レコードのタイトル・デザイン
(C)：Geffen Records

Party Tested
Album Title Treatment
Client: Boardwalk/Pasha
   Records

Party Tested
レコードのタイトル・デザイン
(C)：Broadwalk／Pasha Records

Flora Purim/Airto
Recording Artists Tour Logo
Client: Warner Bros. Records
Art Director: John Cabalka

Flora Purim/Airto
レコーディング・アーティストのツ
アー公演用ロゴ
(C)：Warner Bros. Records
(AD)：John Cabalka.

Carriole
Jean Manufacturer
The translation of "Carriole"
is "horse and carriage."
Client: Chiat Day
Art Director: Brent Thomas

Carriole
ジーンズのメーカー
"Carriole" の意は，「馬と車」であ
る．
（C）: Chiat Day
（AD）: Brent Thomas

CARRIOLE

The Lady And The Clarinet
Stage Play
Client: Mark Taper Forum
Art Director: Liz Kooker

The Lady And The Clarinet
演劇
（C）: Mark Taper Forum
（AD）: Liz Kooker

Rad
Movie Title Treatment
Rad is a movie about BMX
stunt bicycle riding. The
curves and arrows in the logo
suggest the ramps and jumps
involved in these bike con-
tests. I wanted the logo to
convey a sense of movement
and energy.
Client: Ed Thrasher & Assoc.

Rad
映画のタイトル・デザイン
"Rad" はモトクロスの曲乗りの映画
である．ロゴにみられる曲線や矢は
こういったバイクの競技に関係する
坂路やジャンプを想わせている．私
はロゴが活気や勢いのある様を伝え
てくれればと考えた．
(C)：Ed Thrasher & Assoc.

Howie Mandel
Comedian
Howie is famous for wearing
a surgical glove over his head
and inflating it thru his nose.
Client: Warner Bros. Records
Art Director: Jeri McManus

Howie Mandel
コメディアン名
Howie は外科医用の手袋を頭にかぶ
って，これを鼻でふくらませること
ができるので有名である．
(C)：Warner Bros. Records
(AD)：Jeri McManus

Lani Hall
Recording Artist
Client: A&M Records
Art Director: Roland Young

Lani Hall
レコーディング・アーティスト名
(C)：A & M Records
（AD）：Roland Young

Fortune
Recording Group
Client: Warner Bros. Records
Art Director: John Cabalka

Fortune
レコーディング・グループ名
(C)：Warner Bros. Records
（AD）：John Cabalka

Esther Phillips
Recording Artist
Client: Motown Records
Art Director: John Cabalka

Esther Phillips
レコーディング・アーティスト名
(C)：Motown Records
（AD）：John Cabalka

Stevie Wonder

The Secret Life of Plants

**Stevie Wonder, The Secret Life
  Of Plants**
Album Title Treatment
The design was embossed into
the cover of the album. At the
bottom of the cover there was
a description in braille which
explained to a blind person
what a sighted person would
see. The ink had a floral scent
which further enhanced the
album concept.
Client: Motown Records
Art Director: John Cabalka
Illustrator: Margo Z. Nahas

**Stevie Wonder, The Secret Life
  Of Plants**
レコードのタイトル・デザイン
このデザインはレコードのジャケッ
トに型おしされている. ジャケット
のすそ部分に点字の解説があり, 可
視者にどう見えるかを目の不自由な
人に説明するようになっている. 使
用されたインクには花の香りがあっ
て, これが一層このレコードのコン
セプトを高めている.
(C)：Motown Records
(AD)：John Cabalka
(I)：Margo Z. Nahas

Every Wear, Every Where
洋服の会社
クライアントが，社名に関し二転三転していたので，私もデザインの傾向を変え続けるはめになった．最終的に残ったロゴは，通常私がマークに盛りこむより多めの要素をもつデザインになった．しかしこの場合はこうすることが適当だと思えた．
(C)：Breton Industries

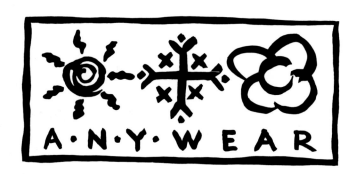

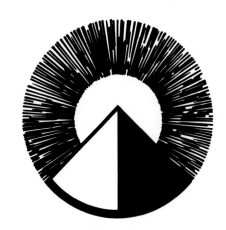

Every Wear, Every Where
Clothing Company
The clients kept changing
their minds about the name of
the company, so I had to keep
changing the direction of the
design. The final logo ended
up with more information
than I normally try to design
into a mark, but it seemed
appropriate in this case.
Client: Breton Industries

Sonheath
音楽出版会社
"Sonheath" は，アメリカン・インデ
ィアンの言葉で"群れの首領"を意
味する．右のページデザインにたど
りつくまでに，私は数種の狼のモチ
ーフを試みてみた．
(C)：Warner Bros. Records
(AD)：John Cabalka

Sonheath
Music Publishing Company
Sonheath is an American
Indian word meaning "leader
of the pack." I experimented
with several wolf motifs
before arriving at the design
on the right.
Client: Warner Bros. Records
Art Director: John Cabalka

Z. Cavaricci
Unisex Clothing Company
The clothing manufactured
by this company had an old
world, Edwardian feeling. I
thought a quill pen drawing
would be appropriate, and
after experimenting with
some heraldic motifs, I stum-
bled on a "Z" shaped dragon.
Client: Z. Cavaricci

Z. Cavaricci
男女兼用の衣料メーカー
この会社で製造している服は，古風
なエドワード調（華美でうっとりす
るような）のものであった．私は羽
ペンで書くのがふさわしいと思い，
紋章のモチーフで幾つか試してみた
後，思いがけず "Z" を型どった竜が
浮かんだのである．
(C)：Z. Cavaricci

Charlie Chan and The Curse
of The Dragon Queen
Movie Title Treatment
The logo I came up with was
a combination of human and
dragon features. I think the
logo was rejected because it
wasn't mainstream enough.
Client: Seiniger & Assoc.
Art Direction: Tony Seiniger

Charlie Chan and The Curse
of The Dragon Queen
映画のタイトル・デザイン
私がいきついたロゴは，人間と竜の
特長を組み合わせたものであった．
私が思うに，これではメインとして
使用するには不向きだったのでこの
ロゴは不採用になったのだろう．
(C)：Seiniger & Assoc.
(AD)：Tony Seiniger

Harmony Pictures
テレビのコマーシャル製作会社
クライアントは，初期のハリウッド
映画のスタジオの雰囲気をもつロゴ
を求めていた．
(C)：Harmony Pictures
(I)：Peter Greco

Harmony Pictures
Television Commercial
  Production Company
The client had requested a
logo with the feeling of an
early Hollywood motion
picture studio.
Client: Harmony Pictures
Illustrator: Peter Greco

FALCONS

Falcons
Football Team Merchandise
Logo
Client: N.F.L. Enterprises

Falcons
フットボールチームの商品用ロゴ
(C)：N.F.L. Enterprises

BLACK 'N BLUE

Black 'N Blue
Recording Group
Client: Geffen Records

Black 'N Blue
レコーディング・グループ名
(C)：Geffen Records

UROK

UROK
Recording Group
Client: FM Music, Ltd.

UROK
レコーディング・グループ名
(C)：FM Music, Ltd.

Spanos
Recording Artist and Album Title Treatment
I designed this logo to look like barbed wire because the artist had a reputation for being a rough and tumble character.
Client: Epic/Pasha Records

Spanos
レコーディング・アーティスト名と
レコードのタイトル・デザイン
このアーティストは荒っぽくて乱雑な性格だという評判だったので, 私はこのロゴを有刺鉄線のように見えるようデザインした.
(C): Epic／Pasha Records

George Benson
Album Title Treatment and
    Tour Logo
The full effect of this logo
can't be appreciated here
because it was embossed
white on white on the album
cover. The logo was so popular with George and his management company that for
three years they used it on all
their tour merchandise.
Client: Warner Bros. Records
Art Director: Richard Seireeni

George Benson
レコードのタイトル・デザインとツ
アー公演用ロゴ
このロゴの効果はここでは十分に味
わうことはできない．というのもこ
のロゴは実際にはレコードジャケッ
ト上で白地に白く浮き出しになって
いるからである．このロゴはGeorge
にも彼の所属会社にも大変好評だっ
たので，３年間も彼らはこのロゴを
ツアー公演用商品全般に使用してい
た．
(C)：Warner Bros. Records
(AD)：Richard Seireeni

Candi's Taking Chances

SCHERRIE
& SUSAYE

Thelma Houston THE DEVIL IN ME

Candi's Taking Chances
Album Title Treatment
Client: Motown Records
Art Director: John Cabalka

Candi's Taking Chances
レコードのタイトル・デザイン
(C)：Motown Records
(AD)：John Cabalka

Scherrie & Susaye
Album Title Treatment
Client: Motown Records
Art Director: John Cabalka

Scherrie & Susaye
レコードのタイトル・デザイン
(C)：Motown Records
(AD)：John Cabalka

Thelma Houston, The Devil
In Me
Album Title Treatment
Client: Motown Records
Art Director: John Cabalka

Thelma Houston, The Devil
In Me
レコードのタイトル・デザイン
(C)：Motown Records
(AD)：John Cabalka

Surfing Robot
紳士用スポーツウェア会社
テクノ・スポーツの発想は，最近迄
流行していた日本製のおもちゃのロ
ボットの影響からくる．
(C)：Gotcha Sportswear

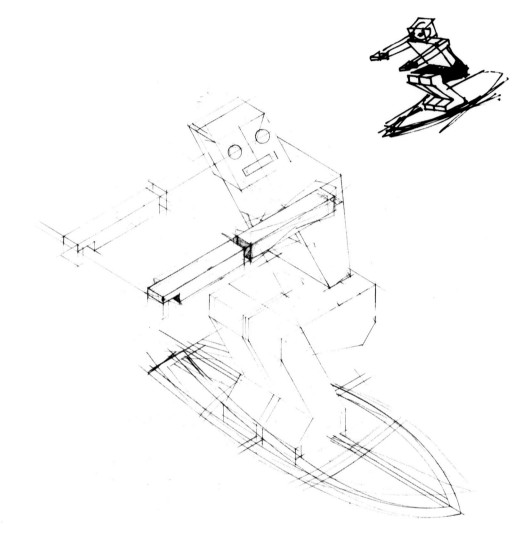

Surfing Robot
Men's Sportswear Company
A techno-sports idea influenced by the recent popularity of Japanese robot toys.
Client: Gotcha Sportswear

Kowabunga Man
Mascot For a Mail-order
 Clothing Catalog
Client: Camp Beverly Hills

Kowabunga Man
通信販売の衣料のカタログ用マスコット
(C)：Camp Beverly Hills

Beach Boy
Men's Sportswear Company
This was a proposed idea for
an up-scale line of designer
beachwear featuring authentic
Hawaiian shirts and accesso-
ries. There was to be a promotional tie-in with the
band of the same name,
The Beach Boys.
Client: Axis Sportswear

Beach Boy
紳士用スポーツウェアの会社
デザイナーによる本物指向のアロハ
シャツと小物を主とした高級ビーチ
ウェア向けに提案されたアイディア.
これには同名のグループ, ビーチ・
ボーイズと販促上のジョイントが見
込まれていた.
(C)：Axis Sportswear

BEACH BOY

Blade Runner
映画のタイトル・デザイン
SF映画のメインタイトル向けに仮
の下絵を書いた．デザインの多くは，
映画のセットのアートディレクショ
ンに影響を受けている．

(C)：Blade Runner Inc.／The Ladd
　　Company

BLADE RUNNER

Blade Runner
Movie Title Treatment
These were preliminary
sketches for a main title treatment of a science fiction
movie. Many of the designs
were influenced by the art
direction of the movie's sets.
Client: Blade Runner Inc./
  The Ladd Company

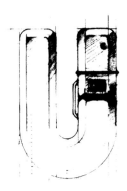

Grasshopper
Album Title Treatment
This was a title design for
a J.J. Cale album cover.
Client: Audigram Records

Grasshopper
レコードのタイトル・デザイン
J. J. Cale のレコードジャケット用
のタイトル・デザイン.
(C)：Audigram Records

Danny DOUMA

Danny Douma
Album Title Treatment
Danny identified with the
aloof confidence of a cat's
personality.
Client: Warner Bros. Records

Danny Douma
レコードのタイトル・デザイン
Danny は，超然とした自信たっぷり
の猫の個性に自らをあてはめていた．
(C)：Warner Bros. Records

Affluence
Swimwear Company
Client: Barely Legal

Affluence
水着の会社
(C)：Barely Legal

Kersz Stout
Artist Representatives
Client: Valerie Kersz and
　　Greg Stout

Kersz Stout
アーティストのレップ
(C)：Valerie Kersz and Greg Stout

Heart
Illustrator's Logo
Client: Margo Z. Nahas

Heart
イラストレーターのロゴ
(C)：Margo Z. Nahas

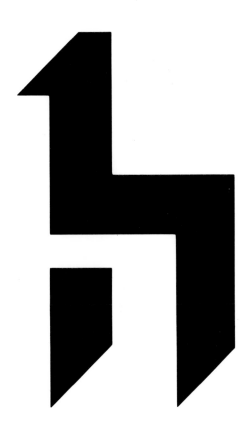

Hirsch Business Interiors
Office Furniture Distributor
This seemed like a natural...a
lower case "h" that happens
to look like a chair.
Client: Ardlo Associates, Inc.

Hirsch Business Interiors
オフィス用家具のディストリビュー
ター
これは無理のない感じの…たまたま
椅子の形に見える小文字の "h" を活
かしたもの.
(C)：Ardlo Associates, Inc.

Tata Vega, Try My Love
Album Title Treatment
Client: Motown Records
Art Director: John Cabalka

Tata Vega, Try My Love
レコードのタイトル・デザイン
(C)：Motown Records
(AD)：John Cabalka

Ronnie Wood
Recording Artist
Illustrator: Margo Z. Nahas

Ronnie Wood
レコーディング・アーティスト名
(I)：Margo Z. Nahas

Mangione
Recording Artist
Client: A&M Records
Art Director: Chuck Beeson

Mangione
レコーディング・アーティスト名
(C)：A & M Records
(AD)：Chuck Beeson

BON·JOVI

Howdy

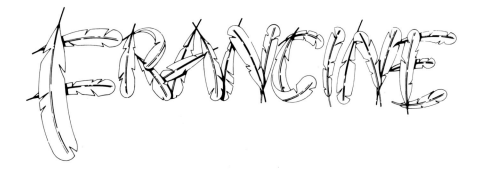

FRANCINE

Bon Jovi
Recording Artist
Client: Polygram Records
Art Director: Bill Levy

Bon Jovi
レコーディング・アーティスト名
(C)：Polygram Records
(AD)：Bill Levy

Howdy
Stationery Design
Client: Vigon Nahas Vigon

Howdy
文房具のデザイン
(C)：Vigon Nahas Vigon

Francine
Article Title Treatment
Client: Chic Magazine
Art Director: Bill Scurski
Illustrator: Margo Z. Nahas

Francine
記事の見出しデザイン
(C)：Chic Magazine
(AD)：Bill Scurski
(I)：Margo Z. Nahas

Miles Ahead
婦人用のスポーツウェア会社
この本が印刷に回された頃，新進の
スポーツウェア会社向けのロゴの下
作業を終えたばかりだった．ここに
あるのはそのアイディアの数点であ
る．クライアントが亀を気にいって
くれればいいのだが．
(C)：Santa Cruz Sportswear

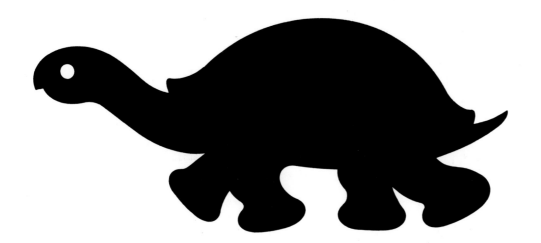

Miles Ahead
Women's Sportswear Company
As this book went to press, we had just completed preliminary work on a logo for a new sportswear company. These were a few of the ideas. I hope they like the turtle.
Client: Santa Cruz Sportswear

Bryant Sterling
Album Title Treatment
This logo was done very early
in my career. My wife rendered
it in pencil because she hadn't
yet mastered the airbrush.
Client: Bryant Sterling
Illustrator: Margo Z. Nahas

Bryant Sterling
レコードのタイトル・デザイン
このロゴは私が仕事を始めたての頃
に作られたもの．妻はまだエアブラ
シを使いこなせなかったので，鉛筆
書きにした．
(C)：Bryant Sterling
(I)：Margo Z. Nahas

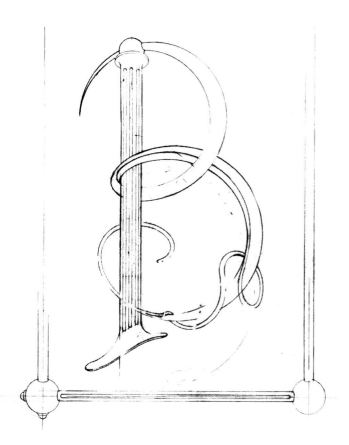

The Letter ''B''
Decorative Alphabet
At one time, I entertained the
idea of doing an alphabet. It
was partially inspired by Erté.
I never found the time to
develop all the letters. This
was a preliminary sketch.
Client: Jay Vigon

The Letter ''B''
飾り文字
ひところ，私はアルファベットに取
りくむことを考えていた．半ば Erté
により着想を得たといえる．全ての
文字についてやるだけの時間はとれ
なかった．これは下絵である．
(C)：Jay Vigon

Return of the Jedi
映画のタイトル・デザイン
この企画に取りかかって大変興奮し
た．というのもスターウォーズの企
画用に採用となるロゴは世界中どこ
でも人目に触れるだろうし，何百と
いう商品にそのロゴが見られるとわ
かっていたからである．これらは仮
の案である．
(C)：Lucasfilm Ltd.

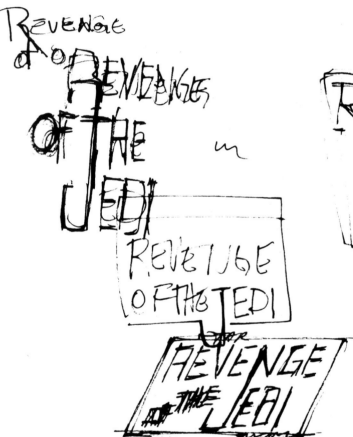

Return of the Jedi
Movie Title Treatment
I was very excitied to work on this project because I knew that an accepted logo for a Star Wars project would be seen everywhere around the world and appear on hundreds of merchandise items. These were some of the preliminary ideas.
Client: Lucasfilm Ltd.

Return of the Jedi
映画のタイトル・デザイン
この映画のタイトルは，はじめ
"Revenge of The Jedi" だったが，
後になって "Return of The Jedi"
に変えられた．いいあんばいに字数
や単語の特徴がごく近いものだった．
(C)：Lucasfilm Ltd.

STAR.WARS

REVENGE OF THE
J E D I

Return of the Jedi
Movie Title Treatment
The original title of this movie was ''Revenge Of The Jedi'' and was later changed to ''Return Of The Jedi.'' Luckily, the number of letters and character of the words was very close.
Client: Lucasfilm Ltd.

Rome Studies Program
ワシントン大学の留学プログラム
大学在学中，私の相棒は建築学のカ
リキュラムの一環として，ローマで
の研究プログラムに参加したことが
ある．我々はこのロゴを大学の建築
学校へ贈呈するつもりで作成したが，
送らずじまいに終わった．
(C)：Vigon Seireeni

Rome Studies Program
University of Washington
 Foreign Studies Program
During college, my partner
had attended a studies pro-
gram in Rome as part of his
Architecture curriculum. We
prepared this logo as a gift to
the University's College of
Architecture but never got
around to sending it to them.
Client: Vigon Seireeni

Loretta Lynn
Country Music Artist
Client: MCA Records
Art Director: Vartan

Loretta Lynn
カントリーミュージックのアーティ
スト名
(C)：MCA Records
(AD)：Vartan

Cheryl and Robert
Wedding Invitation
Client: Cheryl Sindell and
    Robert Heller

Cheryl and Robert
結婚式の招待状
(C)：Cheryl Sindell and Robert
    Heller

Vigon Nahas Vigon
Design Firm
Client: Vigon Nahas Vigon

Vigon Nahas Vigon
デザイン会社
(C)：Vigon Nahas Vigon

Disco
Music Division Logo
Client: Warner Bros. Records
Art Director: John Cabalka

Disco
音楽の部門別用ロゴ
(C)：Warner Bros. Records.
(AD)：John Cabalka

Paul Williams
Album Title Treatment
Client: A&M Records
Art Director: Chuck Beeson

Paul Williams
レコードのタイトル・デザイン
(C)：A & M Records
(AD)：Chuck Beeson

Berkshire
Album Title Treatment
Client: Warner Bros. Records

Berkshire
レコードのタイトル・デザイン
(C)：Warner Bros. Records.

Wave

レストラン・バー

この新しくできた海辺のレストランの名前は元は "Main Street Bar and Grill" であった. 我々はこの名があまりにありふれていると思い, 他の名を考えるから任せてほしいと彼らを納得させた. 彼らの頭を柔らかくさせんとして我々は "Squat 'N Gobble" や "Flaming Colossus" とか "Scotch 'N Penis" といったかなり馬鹿げたアイディアを出した. こうしたお膳立てをし, 我々が一番気に入っていてしかも最もふさわしいと思った名前を彼らに採用させたわけである. "Wave" のためのロゴをデザインするにあたり, 私は海に関するきまりきった表現を避け, それよりも, 想像にまかせる余地を残すような何かをつきつめてみた.

(C) : Michael and Richard Condon and Steve Fargnoli.

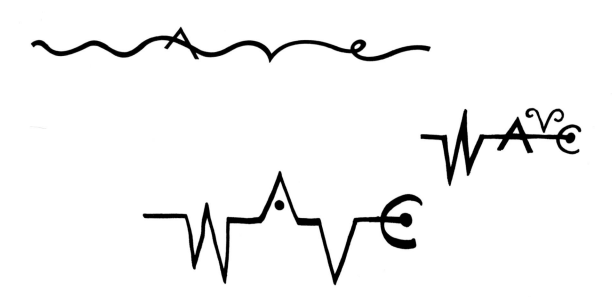

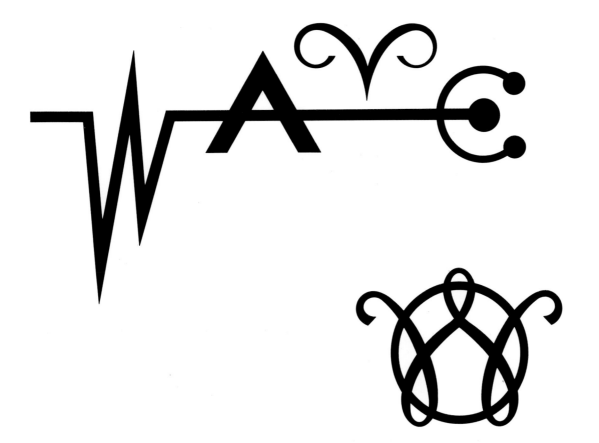

Wave
Restaurant and Bar
The original name for this new, seaside restaurant was ''Main Street Bar and Grill. We thought it was too ordinary and convinced them to let us suggest some alternatives. In an effort to radicalize their thinking, we suggested some very absurd ideas like ''Squat 'N Gobble,'' ''Flaming Colossus'' and ''Scotch 'N Penis.'' This set the stage for them to accept the name we liked best and felt was most appropriate. In designing the logo for ''Wave,'' I avoided nautical clichés and, instead, concentrated on something that left interpretation to the imagination.
Client: Michael and Richard
   Condon and Steve Fargnoli

COSMOPOLIS

Cosmopolis

市民ホール開場記念の夜のイベント
日本の大手衣料会社グループのワール
ド社とその他数社が，1984年，神
戸の市民ホール建設のスポンサーに
なった．Cosmopolis は，マルチ・メ
ディアのオープニングイベントだっ
た．イベントのテーマは未来を楽観
的に視ることに根ざしており，その
未来では人々が平和に暮らし，テク
ノロジーと環境の問題は解決し，世
界中の多様な文化は新たな秩序を成
すよう，異種混合されているのであ
る．このページにあるロゴは，こう
いったテーマを構成する全ての要素
を反映させ，デザインされたもので
ある．右にあるスケッチは，私の仮
のアイディア数点を表している．

(C)：World Co., Japan
(CD)：Shi Yu Chen

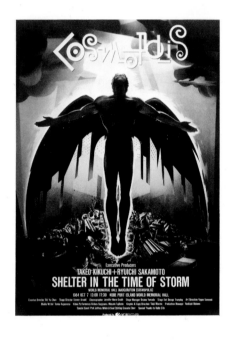

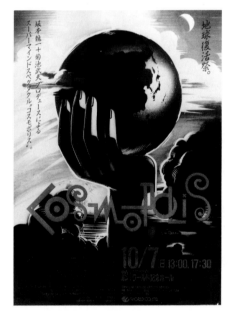

Cosmopolis
Opening Night Event
for a Civic Auditorium
World Company, a large Japanese clothing conglomerate, and several other firms sponsored the construction of a public auditorium in Kobe, Japan in 1984. Cosmopolis was the multi-media opening night event. The theme of the extravaganza was based on an optimistic vision of the future where people lived in peace, where the frictions of technology and environment had been resolved and where the world's diverse cultures had cross-fertilized to form a new order. The logo on the left was designed to reflect all of these theme elements. The sketches on the right represent some of my preliminary ideas.
Client: World Co., Japan
Creative Director: Shi Yu Chen

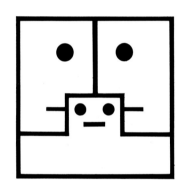

Apollo Ultrapure Water
工業用水の浄化システム・メーカー
ここにあるのは下絵.
(C)：Apollo Ultrapure Water

APOLLO

Apollo Ultrapure Water
Industrial Water Purification
 System Manufacturer
These were preliminary
sketches.
Client: Apollo Ultrapure Water

Apollo Ultrapure Water
工業用水の浄化システム・メーカー
下書きでは，澄んだ水と太陽の神ア
ポロのイメージに私は専念したのだ
が，クライアントは何かもっと奇抜
なものを好んだ．
(C)：Apollo Ultrapure Water

226

Apollo Ultrapure Water
Industrial Water Purification
   System Manufacturer
In the preliminary drawings,
I concentrated on images
of pure water and the god,
Apollo; but the client pre-
ferred something more
whimsical.
Client: Apollo Ultrapure Water

Casadei
礼装用婦人服メーカー
マスター・ロゴとラベルに使用する
デザインの下絵.
(C)：Eletra Casadei

Casadei
Woman's Special Occasion
    Dress Manufacturer
Preliminary sketches for
a master logo and label
applications.
Client: Eletra Casadei

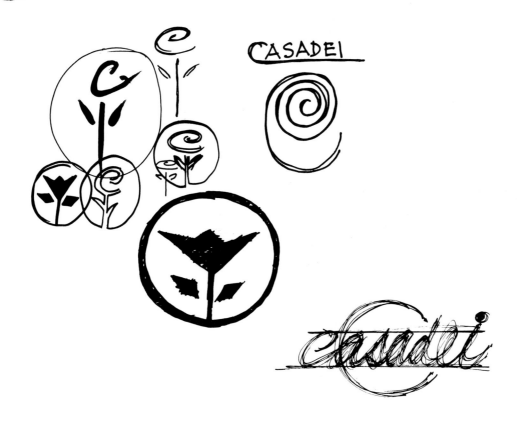

Casadei
礼装用婦人服メーカー
ここにあるロゴは，1962年のピカソ
の彫刻 "Jacqueline Mougins" から
思いついた．右ページの作品はマチ
スの雰囲気を持つものだ．どちらも，
1920年代に広く受け入れられた女
性の美しい姿を捕らえるよう意図さ
れている．
(C)：Eletra Casadei

Casadei
Women's Special Occasion
   Dress Manufacturer
The logo on the left was
inspired by the 1962 Picasso
sculpture, *Jacqueline
Mougins.* The one on the
right had a Matisse feeling.
Both were intended to capture
the prevailing attitudes of fem-
inine beauty in the 1920's.
Client: Eletra Casadei

FLYING
PADRE
PRODUCTIONS

Flying Padre Productions
興行プロダクション
企画によっては，終わらないのでは
ないかと思うものが時としてある．
これはその種の企画だった．いつも
なら2回のプレゼンのところを，こ
のクライアントに対しては5回のプ
レゼンを行った．問題の一部はこの
社名にあった．クライアントはその
響きが気にいったという理由で，古
い映画のくだりからこの名をとった
という．"Flying Padre" 自体はこの
会社の性質について何も表現してい
ないので，私の文字どおりの解釈が
問題を引き起こした．ある絵は，宗
教的であったり，他の絵は飛行にこ
だわりすぎたり，或いはあまりに抽
象的すぎた．
(C)：Mark Romanek

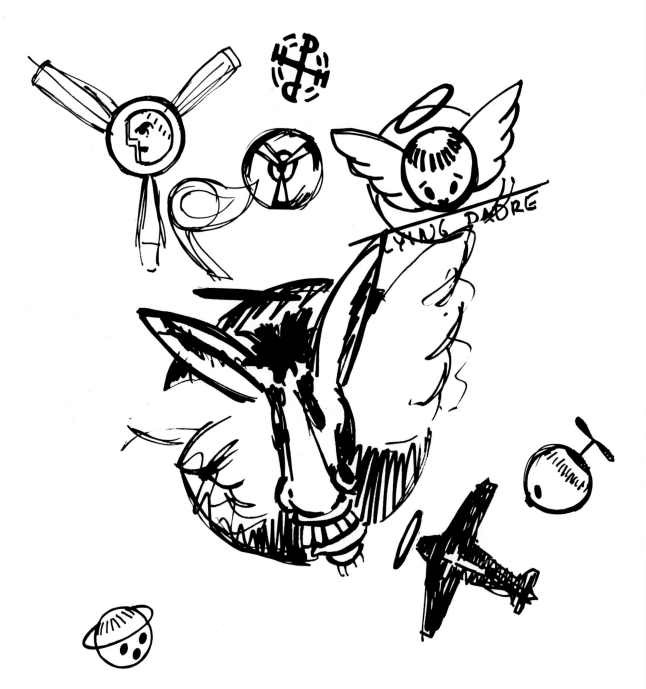

Flying Padre Productions
Entertainment Production
   Company
Sometimes projects seem like
they will never end. This was
one of them. I made five
rounds of presentations to this
client, which is three more
than I usually do. Part of the
problem was in the name. The
client had picked it up from a
line in an old movie because
he liked the sound of it.
Because "Flying Padre" said
nothing about the nature of
the company, my literal interpretations created problems.
Some were too religious.
Others were too aeronautical
or abstract.
Client: Mark Romanek

Flying Padre Productions
興行プロダクション
ここにあるのはクライアントに提示
された後，不採用となった多数のデ
ザインのうち数点．最終的に選ばれ
たデザインは，本の出版時にはでき
あがっていなかった．
(C)：Mark Romanek

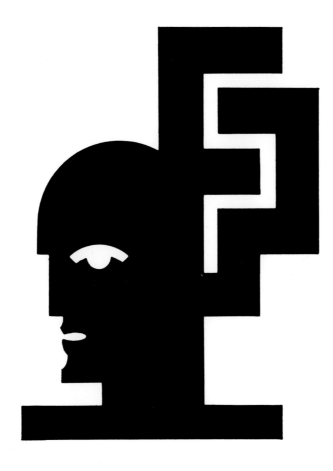

Flying Padre Productions
Entertainment Production
  Company
These are some of the many
designs that were presented to
this client and subsequently
rejected. The design that
was finally chosen was not
completed at the time of
publication.
Client: Mark Romanek

The Prisma Collection
婦人用のスポーツウェア会社
このページにあるロゴは，この企画
で仮提示したものの一部である．採
用となったロゴは右ページの作品．
弧の部分は，見る時間にもよるが，
太陽，もしくは月を表している．波
形の線は水を示している．
(C)：Prisma Corporation

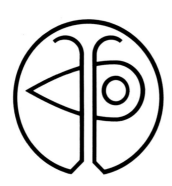

The Prisma Collection
Women's Sportswear Company
The logos on the left were part
of the preliminary presentation on this project. The
approved logo is on the right.
The arc represents the sun or
possibly the moon, depending
on what time you get up. The
wavy line represents water.
Client: Prisma Corporation

Personal Stationary Designs
1979年，私は家族や友人の私用便箋
用にロゴを作ることに決めた．誕生
日やクリスマスに私が贈ったギフト
がこれらのロゴであった．

Personal Stationary Designs
In 1979, I decided to create logos for the personal stationary of some of my family members and friends. They were gifts that I presented on birthdays and Christmas.

Axis
紳士用スポーツウェア会社
紳士用スポーツウェアに組み合わせ
文字を配したロゴの下絵. デザイン
を社名の頭文字に限定するのが自然
なようだった.
(C)：Axis Sportswear

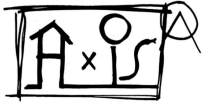

Axis
Men's Sportswear Company
Preliminary sketches for a
logo to be monogrammed on
men's sportswear. It seemed
natural to limit designs to the
initial letter of the company
name.
Client: Axis Sportswear

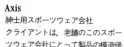

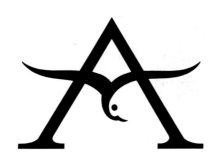

Axis
Men's Sportswear Company
The client had requested a
mark for this previously established sportswear company
that would help prevent product infringements, but he
didn't want an overt design.
The problem called for a dis-
crete solution that could be
tastefully applied to the out-
side of the garments and
would not offend the buyer.
Client: Axis Sportswear

Axis
紳士用スポーツウェア会社
これらは，前ページで示したアイデ
ィアを洗い直した２度目のもの．ク
ライアントは初回のプレゼンで見た
作品よりもあっさりしたものを求め
た．
(C)：Axis Sportswear

Axis
Men's Sportswear Company
These were second round
refinements of the ideas
shown on the previous pages.
The client wanted something
with less volume than he
had seen in the original
presentation.
Client: Axis Sportswear

Crackin
Album Title Treatment
The long curves in some of
the characters suggest a whip.
Client: Warner Bros. Records
Art Director: John Cabalka

Crackin
レコードのタイトル・デザイン
文字の数ヶ所に見られる長い曲線は,
ムチをほのめかしている.
(C)：Warner Bros. Records
（AD）：John Cabalka

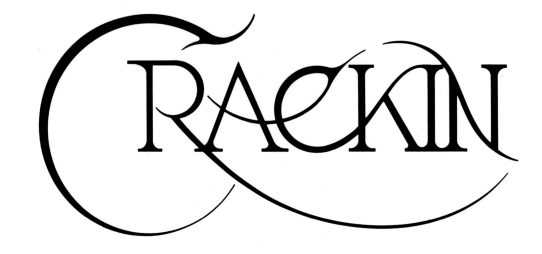

THE FIRST DEADLY SIN

The First Deadly Sin
Movie Title Treatment
This was another of many
proposals for a murder mystery film. The use of fingerprints seemed like an obvious
solution at first, but I don't
recall having ever seen it
used before.
Client: Filmways International
Art Director: Bob Rembert

The First Deadly Sin
映画のタイトル・デザイン
これは，殺人ミステリー映画に対し
数多く提案されたものの１つ．指紋
を使用することが最初は一目瞭然の
とらえ方だと思えたが，私はこの手
法がかつて使われていたのを見かけ
た覚えはない．
(C)：Filmways International
(AD)：Bob Rembert

where Angels
Fear to Tread

Where Angels Fear To Tread
Album Title Treatment
Client: Browning Management

Where Angels Fear To Tread
レコードのタイトル・デザイン
(C)：Browning Management

EAT 'EM AND SMILE

Eat 'Em And Smile
Album Cover Title Treatment
Client: Diamond Dave Enterprises
Warner Bros. Records

Eat 'Em And Smile
レコードジャケットのタイトル・デ
ザイン
(C)：Diamond Dave Enterprises
　　　Warner Bros. Records

SPANOS

Spanos
Album Title Treatment
Client: Epic/Pasha Records

Spanos
レコードのタイトル・デザイン
(C)：Epic/Pasha Records

Zapp II
Album Title Treatment
This album treatment was
inspired by the ''brush stroke''
motifs of Roy Lichtenstein.
Client: Warner Bros. Records
Art Director: Richard Seireeni

Zapp II
レコードのタイトル・デザイン
このレコードのデザインは，Roy
Lichtenstein の "brush stroke"（筆
使い）のモチーフにヒントを得たも
のだ．
(C)：Warner Bros. Records
（AD）：Richard Seireeni

Max Studio
Women's Sportswear Company
This logo was developed as
part of a presentation of fabric
and applique designs. Unfortunately, it was never used.
Client: Leon Max

Max Studio
婦人用スポーツウェア会社
このロゴは，織地とアップリケのデ
ザインを提示する際，その一部とし
て作られたもの．あいにく日の目を
見なかった．
(C)：Leon Max

Why Things Burn
Women's Swimwear
    Manufacturer
The former principals in
another swimwear company
asked us to help launch a new
line. Not only did we design
the logo, but we also came up
with the name.
Client: Pam Feldman and
    Cathy DuPont

Why Things Burn
婦人用水着メーカー
別の水着メーカーの元社長が，新し
いブランド開発に乗り出すので，
我々に手伝うよう要請してきた．
我々はロゴのデザインのみならず，
ブランド名まで思いついてしまった．
(C)：Pam Feldman and Cathy DuPont

Jordan
Logo for my second daughter.
Client: Jordan Halley Vigon

Jordan
私の次女のために作ったロゴ.
(C)：Jordan Halley Vigon

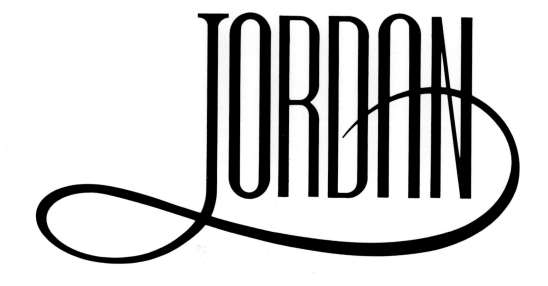

Tamara Gallery
Fine Art Gallery
I intended this logo to be fabricated into a metal sculpture for the front of the gallery.
Client: Robert Bane, Inc.

Tamara Gallery
美術ギャラリー
私はこのロゴがギャラリーの正面を飾るメタル製の彫刻として作り上げられるよう意図した.
(C)：Robert Bane, Inc.

Siren
Film Production Company
The name of this company
was inspired by a description
of the Island of the Sirens in
Homer's·"The Iliad." The
owner of this production firm
likened the film business to
the Siren's song: seductive,
but treacherous.
Client: Julio Caro

Siren
映画製作会社
この社名は，ホメロス作の「イリア
ッド」にでてくる海の精セイレーン
の住む島々の描写から着想を得た．
この製作会社のオーナーは映画の仕
事をセイレーンの歌になぞらえた．
つまり魅力的だが，落とし穴もある
という訳だ．
(C)：Julio Caro

Man Obsessed With V's and S's
Another icon for our agency.
Client: Vigon Seireeni

Man Obsessed With V's and S's
我が社用の別用途のマーク.
(C) : Vigon Seireeni

We would like to thank the following
for their contributions to this project:

Shi Yu Chen
Sarajo Frieden
Christine Karas
Gina Vivona
Dia Eldorado
Richard Hirsch
Ellen Knable
Stat House
Alpha Graphix

MARKS
マークス

1986年 9 月25日　初版第 1 刷発行
1988年 7 月25日　　　第 2 刷発行

定　価　3,800円
著　者　ジェイ・ヴァイゴン©
発行者　久世利郎
印刷所　凸版印刷株式会社
製本所　凸版印刷株式会社
写　植　三和写真工芸株式会社(和文)
発行所　株式会社 グラフィック社
　　　　〒102 東京都千代田区九段北1-9-12
　　　　電話03-263-4318 Fax 03-263-5297
　　　　振替・東京3-114345

ISBN4-7661-0388-2 C3070 ¥3800E